I Want Those Shoes!

Paola Jacobbi

Illustrated by Sujean Rim

SCRIBNER

NEW YORK   LONDON   TORONTO   SYDNEY

SCRIBNER
1230 Avenue of the Americas
New York, NY 10020

First Scribner hardcover edition September 2007

Originally published in Italy in 2004 as *Voglio quelle scarpe!*
by Sperling & Kupfer Editori S.p.A.

Published by arrangement with Sperling & Kupfer Editori S.p.A.

SCRIBNER and design are trademarks of
Macmillan Library Reference USA, Inc., used under license
by Simon & Schuster, the publisher of this work.

For information about special discounts for bulk purchases,
please contact Simon & Schuster Special Sales:
1-800-456-6798 or business@simonandschuster.com.

Designed by Davina Mock-Maniscalco
Text set in Adobe Garamond

Manufactured in the United States of America

1   3   5   7   9   10   8   6   4   2

Library of Congress Cataloging-in-Publication Data
Jacobbi, Paola.
[Voglio quelle scarpe! English]
I want those shoes! / Paola Jacobbi.—1st Scribner ed.
p. cm.
Includes bibliographical references.
1. Women's shoes. 2. Women's shoes—Social aspects. I. Title.
GT2130.J3413 2007
391.4'13—dc22
2006035880

ISBN-13: 978-0-7432-7774-7
ISBN-10:   0-7432-7774-0

This book is dedicated to women, who understand.
And also to men, who don't.
But who, in the end, grow to appreciate.

Contents

The madness of women,
That need for shoes
That will hear no reason.
What do millions matter
When in exchange you have shoes?

—Elio e le Storie Tese, "La follia della donna"

I Want Those Shoes!

Introduction

Five years ago, I moved into my current apartment. The previous tenant, the usual friend of a friend, was a very sporty type, with a decided flair for DIY. While showing me the features of the house, he paused proudly before a recess in the wall that he had skillfully transformed into a spacious cupboard replete with shelves, where he kept his numerous mountaineering sweaters (he's not the jacket and tie sort).

At the sight of this, I was filled with excitement, and cried out: "How wonderful! That's where I can store my shoes!"

He stared at me in amazement, and asked: "Well, how many shoes do you own? I myself own four: two for the winter, and two for the summer!"

If ever I had doubted it, here was the proof: men and women are very different in several respects, but the moment you get onto the subject of shoes, a chasm opens between the two sexes.

It has been calculated that the average person walks almost two thousand miles during their lifetime. Thus, shoes are useful objects for both sexes, but it is only for women that they become an all-consuming obsession. Women's magazines tell us how to use shoes to find ourselves a husband, reconquer a lost lover, or get that job we hanker after.

They can cost a fortune; yet while money itself does not bring happiness, a pair of new shoes can bring about a kind of exaltation that comes pretty close to that fleeting pleasure described by the philosophers. The reason is often a mystery. One explanation may be that, unlike many other objects—clothes, for example—shoes have a distinct advantage. Whether you're fat or thin, short or tall, beautiful or ugly, you can buy all the shoes your heart desires.

Shoes possess magical properties; capable of making you feel splendid or sexy, elegant or sporty at a single stroke. In spite of the soles coming into contact with the less-than-immaculate streets, and indeed our own sweat, they remain works of art—or at least of a kind of noble craftsmanship, which at the end of the day is not that far removed from that of jewelry. With the difference that they cost somewhat less than diamonds, which are considered to be "a girl's best friend." In the end that's what shoes are: our best friends.

At this point I have to come clean and admit that the aim of this book is not to arrive at a definitive understanding of the subject, because that would be impossible. The French director François Truffaut maintained that cinemagoers have two professions: their own as well as that of film critic. In just the same way, all women are experts on shoes.

They always have been, but over the last ten years this phenomenon has increased massively due to several factors. In order to increase the popularity of their brands, the great fashion houses have invested a great deal in the production of accessories—not only shoes but bags, glasses, and cosmetics, all of which are in a far more affordable price range than clothes, suits, and coats.

For a long time, the obsession with luxury shoes has been the prerogative of a select caste composed of "It Girls," the females of the international jet set, a select tribe of actresses, socialites, and millionairesses whose members could be identified by the accessories with which they adorned themselves. Their distinguishing tattoos were the labels—Hermès, Gucci, Caovilla, Ferragamo, Blahnik—which they procured by putting their names down on the special waiting lists of international boutiques.

Subsequently, in accordance with the new commercial politics of the top brands, what was once the preserve of an elite has now turned into a behavioral trend for the masses. The brands have multiplied or branched out into numerous lines, along with their collector-buyers.

Over the last couple of years, producers have described the state of the shoe market as being critical, as is the case with other fashion sectors: decreasing exports, an increase in imports of mass-produced, shoddier goods from China, Vietnam, and India. And yet, in spite of these intimations of economic crisis, or perhaps precisely because of them, a pair of high-quality shoes continues to be seen as a form of intelligent investment, partly due to the philosophy of "spending more to spend less," partly because a pair of designer shoes is one of the most widespread status symbols to be found, and one that is most difficult to renounce. For those people unable to afford the hot new pieces of a collection, there exist stores, outlets, and markets where at a far lower price, one can easily pick up models that certainly haven't yet lost their luster.

Perhaps, in order for shoes to once more become truly exclusive objects, we will have to return to made-to-measure products, as happened before World War II. It's not a coincidence that in London, if you're a little bit handy, there now exists a two-day shoe-manufacturing course from Prescott & Mackay (for further information see the Web site, www.prescottandmackay.co.uk).

Frankly, I don't believe that this initiative will be particularly successful. The attraction of shoes rests entirely in the encounter: there they lie, splendid, virginal, on show for all to see, whether in a well-illuminated city center shop or jumbled up on a pile in a market stall.

A shoe, just like love, can awaken violent instincts. I have seen things that men could never even believe possible, but which women have experienced, often in first person: fisticuffs for the last pair of leopard-skin shoes in a size 7; elbow jabs to get to a ridiculous pair of gold sandals; even insults exchanged over an absolutely ordinary-looking pair of brown ankle boots and shame that everyone wanted them.

Our passion for shoes has an extraordinary history behind it. Mankind remained barefoot for precious little time. Already in certain prehistoric graffiti one can make out footwear derived from animal skins. The evolution of shoes proceeded apace alongside fashion and customs.

Finally, here is my own personal "shoeography." I wrote the book you are now holding in your hands while wearing almost exclusively a pair of Nike Pegasus, the same sneakers I use for jogging. For me, it is the equivalent of being barefoot.

Wandering around the city in search of inspiration, looking in shop windows, and making special note of the shoes women were walking around in, I was never without my pair of black, medium-heeled, slightly pointed brushed calfskin boots, one of my most successful purchases of the winter 2002–2003. They taught me one thing: what you're looking for is not always on display, even in the better-stocked shops. Carefully explain to the assistant what it is you're after. In the storeroom there might lie—as was the case with my beloved boots—the exact design you're looking for, but which, thanks to the mysterious rules of fashion, might not fit into the trend of the moment.

When I went to interview Sara Porro, one of the best shoe designers around, I made the great mistake of wearing an old pair of Hogan suede lace-up ankle boots (it was freezing cold!). Being a kind of high priestess of elegant footwear, she gave me a filthy look, but she charmingly forgave me.

On the other hand, for my trip to the Ferragamo museum in Florence, I wore a pair of Dolce & Gabbana shoes from the 2000 collection in patent leather and snakeskin, with an ankle strap and fairly low heel, which had become quite comfortable through intensive use. This too was a bit of a gaffe, but the best I could do under the circumstances, in view of the intense day I had ahead of me. They too were kind enough not to comment—thanks for that!

In order to celebrate the end of this marvelous journey into an obsession—mine and others'—for shoes, I haven't yet decided which shoes to wear. I might go and buy a new pair for the occasion. In fact, come to think of it, I really need some.

Women Who Talk
with Their Feet
(and Run on Heels)

There is a story told of certain Neapolitan politicians in the 1950s who used to present potential voters with the gift of a single shoe. After the voting had taken place, they would complete the pair. A pair of shoes is, indeed, a perfect metaphor for a couple, as is sadly emphasized by the expression adopted by many abandoned women: "He tossed me aside like an old shoe"—a single shoe being the ultimate in unusable objects. When there's only one left behind, there really is no difference between a woman and a shoe.

In Italian, we have the expressions "to talk with one's feet," "to write with one's feet," or "to act with one's feet," in other words, to do something very badly or carelessly, lacking all skill, tact, or expertise. The negative connotation derives from the contrast between (noble) hands and (ignoble) feet. It's an archaic view of the hands as being nearer to the mind and the heart, while feet remain down below, mere brainless means of transport.

In English, however, it is crystal clear that shoes (and by extension the feet contained within them) are the foundations of the personality of the person who is wearing them. "Putting oneself in someone's shoes," would be "wearing someone's clothes" in Italian. As is often the case, the English language is more efficient than Italian. Think about it: putting oneself in someone's shoes is truly an intimate gesture, far more so than borrowing some clothes.

3

For women, in particular, it is so intimate as to be one of our first actions after learning to stand up and walk. As soon as we want to feel "grown up," we slip on a pair of our mother's shoes, preferably high-heeled ones. In so doing, we climb onto a pedestal that instantly heightens our sense of what it is to be female. However fleetingly, those "borrowed" shoes make us grow in every sense of the word.

While psychoanalysts describe this as an act of "projection," I remember it being a magical moment. All dressing-up games originate from this gesture.

For adults, the sight of a little girl in high-heeled shoes is both tender and comical; for the child, however, it marks entry into a world of aspirations and dreams. The sensation of our chubby little legs wandering around in the same shoes in which Mommy herself walks creates the illusion that soon we too will be able to do "grown-up" things.

Sigmund Freud would argue that the child's appropriation of the maternal shoes almost constitutes a seduction ploy aimed at the father, a little girl's attempt to assume the mother's role.

And then what happens? You grow up, you get to be the same size as Mommy, and your individual personality begins to assert itself with the first independent purchase of shoes. As adults, we ask shoes to be our representatives. The beauty of it is that they needn't permanently define us. At any given moment of our lives, and even in a single day, shoes are indicators of our age, mood, and desires. Shoes say everything about a woman.

The actress Penelope Cruz confesses: "I have never been able to study a new role until, along with the director, we choose the shoes the woman we are about to bring to the screen will be wearing. Everything starts down there."

So, the question is: What *do* women say when they talk with their feet?

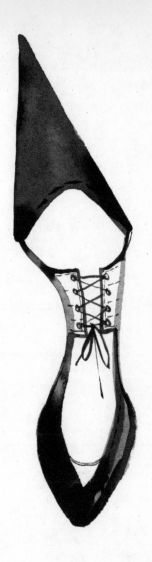

Sex and the Shoe

Women's shoes, more than anything else, speak the language of sex.

You don't have to be a moralist/fetishist like Nanni Moretti (picture the procession of feet in the film *Bianca*) nor, with respect, the anthropologist Desmond Morris, in order to understand the message transmitted by a girl in a pair of silent, rubber-soled loafers versus one wearing noisy stilettos. But that's only a first impression. That old chestnut (heels = sex goddess, flats = nun) is constantly challenged by variations in fashion and customs. And yet, one thing remains certain: a high-heeled shoe is the one object of apparel that—more than any other—marks the difference between the male and female of our species.

Just to get things straight: Have you ever seen a transsexual in pumps? And, for all the talk about Millennium Man being a narcissist and a flirt, he's yet to be spotted in a pair of stilettos. Men have said yes to mascara on their eyelashes, eye shadow on their eyelids, and even to the fiendishly painful practice of waxing; but they haven't yet begun to wear stilettos, as least outside of cross-dressing-themed gay parties.

Who knows, though, it might yet happen. For the ever-growing number of "metrosexual" men, those who are inspired by the fashion proclivities of a figure like David Beckham, that day could come sooner rather than later. (And will signal a period of collective mourning for us women, and will be the subject of an entirely different book.) For now, at least, it is out of the question.

Stilettos are girls' stuff. The higher and pointier the heels, the more they are seen as a symbolic declaration of our power and diversity, and therefore the more they are blatantly provocative. "Mine are higher than yours," is what those clickety-clacking women in streets and offices are really saying. Yup, that's their message to women they're competing with, and, above all, to the men with whom they're engaged in either love or war.

Surely it's no coincidence, either, that, from Cinderella onward, the popular female narrative has been greatly concerned with shoes. Prince Charming is bagged thanks to a pair, be they the glass slippers (clearly a symbol of virginity) belonging to the chaste Cinderella, or a pair of stilettos worn by the metropolitan predators of *Sex and the City*, whose characters share two great weaknesses: men and shoes.

In this instance, too, shoes are an integral part of the characters' personalities. "Sometimes, when we're about to shoot a close-up, the director will say to me that I can take off my shoes, seeing as my feet won't be in the frame," says Sarah Jessica Parker. "But I've never done it; the expression of a woman in flats is totally different from one in heels."

This is a truth that hasn't escaped Patricia Field, wardrobe stylist of *Sex and the City*, who created a new modern cult out of the dazzling designer shoes and clothes worn by the women in the show.

The cream of the crop, as far as the shoes are concerned, are undoubtedly the Manolo Blahniks—a brand that is to shoes what Ferrari is to luxury cars. In one episode, Carrie gets lost and ends up in an alleyway, face-to-face with a mugger. She begs him, "Take my bag, my ring, my watch, but leave me my Manolos!" This paradoxical one-liner hints at a new scale of values—which is probably why it has become so well known, at least among *Sex and the City* aficionados.

In another episode, Carrie attends a baby shower. Concerned about dirt and germs her guests might carry on their soles, the hostess asks the guests to remove their shoes before entering her apartment. At the end of the afternoon, Carrie can't find her Manolos: they've been nicked by a magpie, attracted by their beauty and sparkle.

Having shoes as the protagonists of such a popular TV show has transformed a secret label known to only a few privileged fashion insiders into a mass myth—at least as far as its followers are concerned: you can't buy a pair of Manolos for less than $400!

The Blahnik brand has even penetrated the world of rap music. In Jay-Z's song "Bonnie and Clyde," dedicated to his pop star girlfriend, Beyoncé Knowles, the rap artist promises to love and cherish his woman by offering her an Hermès "Birkin" bag, a Mercedes Benz, and a pair of Manolos.

Manolo Blahnik, the man behind the label, was born in the Canary Islands in 1943. After studying fine art and architecture, in the early 1970s he moved to New York, where he met Diana Vreeland, the legendary editor of *Vogue,* who encouraged him to design shoes. His first devotees were the most glamorous actresses of the age: Marisa Berenson, Jane Birkin, Charlotte Rampling. Today his shoes can be found not only in high-class boutiques and on the feet of celebrities such as Kate Moss and Jennifer Aniston, but also in design museums.

Manolo's comment on the lengths people will go to for a pair of his shoes, and for shoes in general, is: "Women love transforming themselves, and shoes are the quickest and easiest way for them to achieve instant metamorphosis. And they cost less than a piece of jewelry, or an haute-couture frock."

Another high-profile designer of sexy shoes who has come to the fore in recent years is Jimmy Choo. His brand is so popular that in British bingo halls, the number 32 is now made to rhyme with Jimmy Choo. Tamara Mellon, the owner of the company that names actresses such as Halle Berry and Catherine Zeta-Jones among its devotees, declared: "The amazing popularity of accessories in recent years can easily be explained. People these days dress in a way that's increasingly unstructured and casual. Bags, and above all shoes, are all that remain to add a sexy touch to a person's look."

In Italy, one of great producers of shoes that are both sexy and, according to those in the know, comfortable, is Sergio Rossi, which today is part of the Gucci group. Another skillful artisan specializing in "precious" shoes is René Fernando Caovilla, who happens to be a Venetian in spite of his bullfighter's name. His creations almost exclusively feature vertiginously high heels and are highly decorative and very, very sexy. Caovilla says: "I don't make shoes to be worn every day to the office, they are prized objects which celebrate female beauty." They are erotic objects, worn in order to be discarded at the threshold of the bedroom. And in fact, a pair of luxury stilettos is the stuff of fetishists' dreams, as the proliferation of porn Web sites dedicated to the lower female extremities testifies.

It was Freud who drew our attention to the fact that the foot is a full-blown erogenous zone, complete with highly sensitive nerve endings, and that fetishism is not so much a perversion as one element of an erotic relationship in which the person is substituted for an object. Fetishism is an extreme fantasy, at times an indicator of incomplete sexuality. As Karl Kraus put it in one of his memorable aphorisms: "There is no more unhappy being than a fetishist who yearns for a female shoe, and has to make do with the complete woman." At other times, however, fetishism is merely one of many innocent seduction games in which the man watches and the woman acts, walking in her heels while putting herself through exquisite torture.

Torture like the kind self-imposed by the heroic Italian

soubrette Simona Ventura, who spent five hours of live coverage of the Sanremo music festival perched on a pair of sparkly sandals with murderous four-and-a-half-inch heels. At the end of this tour de force, the poor creature muttered to her pan-European audience: "My feet are like a pair of sausages."

Mocassino Comodino
(The Comfortable Loafer)

In Spain, the gossips of the *prensa del corazón* recount how Letizia Ortiz, the television journalist and their future queen, didn't wear heels before she met Prince Felipe. From that day onward, she never wore anything less than three and a half inches in order to reach the height of His Highness. Before that, however, Letizia was often seen wearing loafers—no doubt because loafers are comfortable shoes par excellence, the footwear of choice for the woman who has her head screwed on and plenty to get done; the woman who drives, who is athletic, and who has no time for frivolous pursuits. However, above all, they are for middle-class women who have grown up in circles where the very sight of a high-heeled shoe is considered "vulgar," and where even the most oblique reference to sex is kept quiet for the sake of discretion.

And what could be more discreet than a pair of loafers? Loafers are the modern-day equivalent of moccasins (an Algonquian word meaning a low-cut shoe created from a single piece of folded leather), which were worn by Native American Indians and Eskimos. Colonial settlers who arrived in those lands wearing European shoes ill suited to the terrain immediately adopted them. Over time, slight differences between one model and another came to signify members of the various tribes.

Today things are not that different. The urban prairie teems with loafers, each one indicating a particular way of defining comfort.

One of the most recent styles are JPs, by Tod's, the ones with the little balls on the sole. They were created by Diego Della Valle in 1979, and became almost a symbol of the 1990s. You could say that this design relaunched the loafer, transforming it from a fusty object to a fashionable shoe to the point where it became, in its various guises and seasons, a status symbol for the middle class. In the summer of 2004, Tod's managed to achieve a kind of squaring of the circle by putting heels on their loafers. Not ordinary, visible heels, which would create a boring governessy look, but a little hidden elevation within the shoe itself. It provided a kind of "doping" so as not to be a completely flat shoe, which many women don't care for.

Innovations apart, the traditional "balled loafers" are for ladies on wheels who spend their days accompanying their children from tennis to karate, from German lessons (*Cara*, we're Europeans now, this is the language of the future) to piano lessons. They're busy moms who often drive station wagons with automatic gear shifts, so as to have one arm free to thump their offspring: these women don't need the elevation of heels, as the role of manager of their families has already brought them to the top of their game.

Then there are the "Rising Super-Grannies," fiftysomethings who have always invested in long-lasting shoes for reasons of domestic economy. And nothing, in their eyes, is more long-lasting than a loafer with a Gucci gold horse-bit ornament. They've been wearing them since the 1970s; often they own an entire collection in different colors and finishes. They wear them to lunch with their friends, to play with their grandchildren, and to reproach their daughters, who, for some unknown reason, prefer athletic shoes, which they consider a reprehensible choice.

The Milanese Rising Super-Grannies abandon their Gucci loafers only during the annual summer exodus to Santa Margherita:

in Liguria they prefer wearing sailing shoes, Top-Siders, or Sebagos to accompany their husbands to the harbor. There they stay for an aperitif with the other wives while the men throw themselves into watching and discussing Paul Cayard for the entire weekend.

In wintertime, these ladies repair to Courmayeur, where, to receive their friends, they pull out of the cupboard a slipperlike alternative: Belgian loafers, inspired by the traditional footwear of Flanders peasants. Made of felt, with leather trimmings and a little tassel in the center, these loafers ensure that the lady of the house always has a smile on her face. If the lady is leftward-leaning, and the house in question is not the family apartment in Val d'Aosta but instead a radical-chic farmhouse in Tuscany, she will be wearing a pair of colored velvet slippers known as *friuliane*.

Another fan of comfortable footwear is the ultratraditional woman. She has always chosen what are known as penny loafers, the most classic loafers in the world. When she was young she wore them with a coin in the groove, blushing at the idea of wearing the penny on the right or the left to indicate whether she was single or already taken. Later she got married in a downtown church, and when cracks began to appear in the marriage, she consoled herself by moving on from penny loafers to loafers with high, clumpy heels—an utter abomination. In fact, the husband ended up eloping with the baby-sitter.

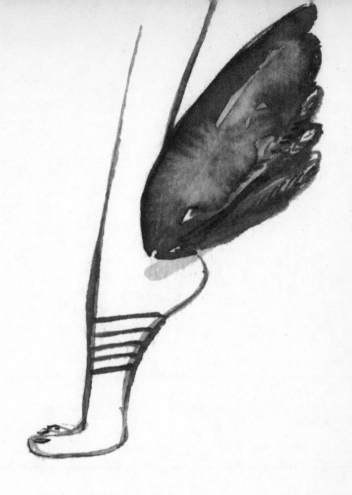

Athletic Shoes:
Not Just for Sport

The story of rubber-soled shoes originates in America. Toward the end of the nineteenth century, these shoes were the preserve of the rich, who wore them for elitist sports such as croquet or tennis. The first mass-produced model saw the light of day in America in 1917; they were called—and indeed are still called—Keds. Two years later, Converse All-Stars, which laced up to the ankle, came along. They were suitable for "street" sports such as basketball. The same model is still in production.

More than just comfortable, in fact *extremely* comfortable, this type of footwear which was originally designed for sports, is now recommended by all orthopedic specialists to avoid corns and other deformations of the foot. In appearance at least, the sneaker is pretty standard, it's almost a "nonshoe." Being unisex, it cannot add inches to one's height, and the shape is always more or less the same. What do vary are colors, brands, and certain optional extras that differentiate between styles. Nike, with their "springs" (Shox, Fsm) are radically different from a pair of Adidas designed by the Japanese designer Yohji Yamamoto, much loved by fashion victims the world over.

There are those of us who buy a new pair each season (with the excellent excuse that all trainers recommend replacing sports shoes after a while due to the fact that, like used car tires, a worn sole loses its tread and cannot hold the road), and those who get attached to a particular model continue to search for it even after it is no longer produced in their own country.

Among sneaker addicts, for example, there is a subgroup consisting of fans of the Nike Silver, a shoe characterized by a pattern of silver light-reflecting bands, which are also said to be perfect for winter, being snug, warm, and soft. Unfortunately, in the last year they've been "chilled down," in other words produced in an even more high-tech and therefore lighter material, which renders them less versatile when it comes to the changing seasons.

Be they "technical" or "designer," athletic shoes have become the leisure shoes of choice, transmitting entirely different messages depending on who wears them and on what occasion. Whether you like them or not, they too have become a fetish.

The sponsors of this development are sports celebrities (obvious) but also luminaries from the world of entertainment (less obvious). Music, in particular hip-hop culture, has launched and continues to launch ever newer and hipper models of athletic shoes (a rapper wearing loafers or Church's brogues is a rare sight indeed!), which are immediately taken up by tribes of urban young people the world over.

In reality, show business has appropriated and, in its turn, taken to the limit a trend that is well established among ordinary people: an ever-increasing attention to physical fitness and as a consequence the foot apparel necessary to obtain and maintain it. Here is a statistic that says it all: in the 1950s in the United States, less than 40 million pairs of sports shoes were sold. Today we're at more than 350 million.

During this boom, the Nike brand (which was born in 1972, but has gone stratospheric over the last ten years) comfortably dominated the 1990s thanks to avant-garde methods of communication, while the 1980s were epitomized by Reebok (born in 1982), the shoe of choice for practitioners of Jane Fonda's aerobic workouts and the first shoes specifically designed for a female foot. A flagbearer for Reebok was Melanie Griffith in the film *Working*

Girl. The film showed a New York commuter arriving at work wearing sneakers, which she then slips into her bag and replaces with traditional heels. The fashion of using two pairs of shoes for the double life of the commuter is in decline but has not entirely vanished. In March 2004, the American monthly magazine *Lucky* carried out a survey amongst its readers. To the question "Do you change your shoes when you walk into the office?" 62.4 percent replied no, while a respectable 37.6 percent replied in the affirmative. The most telling truth to emerge from this is that women of the new era have a sense of practicality, and no intention of giving up either comfort or style.

The new millennium opened with a film that symbolized a breaking away from Hollywood's cultural norm and offered an entirely new concept of what sporting apparel can represent. The film was *The Royal Tenenbaums,* directed in 2001 by Wes Anderson. At the very moment when Nike was reaching the pinnacle of its success, conquering ever greater chunks of the market, Wes Anderson was bringing to our attention three sportswear brands (not just shoes) that at the time seemed completely out of fashion: Adidas, Fila, and Lacoste. Each character in the film was assigned one of these three brands by the director-scriptwriter.

The brainy elder brother (Ben Stiller) was an Adidas aficionado, his neurotic poetess sister (Gwyneth Paltrow) wore only Lacoste, and the jock brother (Luke Wilson) in Fila perfectly cloned the look of Bjorn Borg, uncontested tennis champion of the late 1970s and early 1980s.

The Royal Tenenbaums, which in appearance at least was highly surreal, was not entirely divorced from reality, as it presaged the crisis in the Nike brand, under fire both from antiglobalization movements as well as the fickle caprices of consumers. Today, at least from a communications perspective, Nike is increasingly trying to play on its strengths as a high-tech product for real athletes or wannabe-athletes with the promise of extraordinary sporting performances. It's not a coincidence that the name of one of their latest models plays on the concept of speed: it is called Nike Shox Turbo.

Among Nike's burgeoning rivals, it is worth mentioning the rebirth of Puma, which, while scarcely touching the original 1960s design, has bounced back into fashion and was the first to conquer the skateboarding tribes. Pumas appear somewhat low-tech, simple in design, more suitable for wearing to a party than attempting to emulate the sporting prowess of the Beckham-Totti-Ronaldo triad. In other words, they do not appear to be part of that ever-more-pervasive equation: superstar athletes + multi-national sponsor = success. Nonetheless, during the Iraqi conflict pacifist groups on the Internet invited people to boycott Nike in favor of the trendy and (above all) German Puma brand, which originated in a country that refused to support George W. Bush.

Another brand which has attacked Nike "from the left corner," so to speak, is Adidas, with its Gazelle model, in particular, an evocative, low-tech name for a style that has become the strolling shoe of choice for the Happy Hour brigade in many cities, such as Paris and Milan.

Another brand enjoying a fashion moment is ASICS, which for many years has been living in the shadows. Testimony (or testimonial, we'll never know) of a growing interest in Asian martial arts, Quentin Tarantino's film *Kill Bill* showcases the actress Uma Thurman with a pair of yellow ASICS, the Onitsuka Tigers, on her feet. Originally created for practitioners of tai chi, they became an overnight cult classic.

Until the next new athletic shoe comes along, of course.

A Republic Founded on Shoes

Winter 2004. A verbal battle of personal attacks on the stage of the Italian parliament. The Honorable Gabriella Carlucci (Center Right) is mocked for her kinky stilettos. All hell breaks loose. Carlucci defends herself, crying, "I refuse to relinquish my femininity for the sake of politics. The Left won't let go of the battles of the past where in order to prove their worth young girls had to cover themselves up in bulky, mannish clothes. Now we are the truly liberated women: wearing makeup, stylishly dressed with our stiletto heels. We are the new frontier of female emancipation."

The Honorable Rosy Bindi (Center Left, in the habit of wearing low oxfords) rebuts, "Please! Let's not turn things on their head. They are the ones who want to discriminate, not us, by trying to impose their stereotype of femininity."

According to the Right, the high heel represents freedom of expression because it signifies not being afraid of passing for a fool. The high heel is a form of slavery, and liberates only those not wearing it, says the Left. The debate remains ongoing; to tell the truth, it may never be resolved. Italy, a country shaped like a boot, whose national sport is football (played with the foot), has two great passions: politics and shoes. We have the greatest shoe manufacturers in the world, and a bit of name-calling and finger-pointing between the Right and the Left won't be denied to anyone, whether in bars, living rooms, or even at the family Christmas lunch.

The point is, tell me what shoes you wear and I'll tell you who you voted for.

Today the politics of footwear are somewhat more subtle (ideologies and walls didn't fall in vain), but during the 1970s or "Years of Lead," a period in Italy of stark extremes when the Left and Right were locked in bitter, often violent conflict, it was very easy to distinguish "companions" from "fascists."

Left-leaning boys wore the immortal Clarks desert boots. Recently we have seen them on the feet of the so-called *giratondini,* or anti-Berlusconi protestors; though, given the average age of Nanni Moretti and his cohorts, these are the same young people of yesteryear who simply remained loyal to both footwear and flag.

In the 1970s, girls from the Left pounded the streets in (highly uncomfortable) Dutch clogs, and went camping in espadrilles. Their only concession to sex appeal was the high-heeled version of espadrilles, which laced around the calf, and which made anything less than perfect legs look like mortadella sausages encased in netting.

Right-wing boys, on the other hand, favored Barrow's, a pointy-toed English shoe that peeked out from the hem of their flares, while the right-wing girls couldn't live without their Gucci loafers with gold horse bits, the same shoes their mothers wore and never ceased wearing (see the earlier chapter on loafers).

In the 1980s, during the hedonistic Reagan years, Timberland boots arrived in Italy and instantly became the footwear of choice for the *paninari,* or "sandwich eaters," the new generation of young people who had been so traumatized by events of the previous decade that they wanted nothing more to do with politics. Timberlands were originally American foresters' shoes, and they provided an ideal link between a kind of "frontier and wide-open spaces" culture and a world of new urban habits and customs. Fast food restaurants, introduced in Italy during this period, were the headquarters of *paninari* gatherings in the big cities.

Nowadays, Timberlands fall into the category of leisure shoes worn during cold weather in the fresh air; they've been stripped of all "frontier" associations.

In the meantime, antiglobalization movements have demonized fast food chains for a number of reasons: economic issues related to the unions (exploitation of low-cost workforce), cultural issues (standardizing "tastes" across the world), and philosophical-foodie concerns (to reduce dependence on meat in the face of emerging validation of vegetarian diets, due in part to the spread of Asian and New Age philosophies).

One of the rallying points for the antiglobalization movements is the battle against the big international brands: indeed, one of the most hated is Nike itself, which has been targeted both by Naomi Klein, author of the seminal tract, *No Logo: No Space, No Choice, No Jobs,* as well as the militant documentary maker Michael Moore in his 1997 film *The Big One.* Both are cultural icons among the demonstrators who brought chaos to American campuses toward the end of the 1990s, organizing sit-ins to boycott Nike products in shopping centers.

After September 11, 2001, this kind of action quieted down, at least in its more spectacular forms, but it left traces in people's consciences. "No Global" young people have a fondness for Campers, a Spanish brand of shoes that play the irony card (on some models, for example, the left foot is different from the right.) Created from rough-and-ready or even recycled materials, Campers are the nearest thing we have to the ideals of the fashion-conscious nature lover: a marriage of ethics and aesthetics. True purists, however, reject all brands.

Mostly, however, people resign themselves to wearing what they like and what they happen to find. A politically correct shoe has not yet been invented. Whoever manages to come up with one will be the Bill Gates of the next century.

The Imelda Syndrome

In 1986, as she fled the Philippines for exile in Hawaii, Imelda Romuáldez Marcos, wife of the dictator, Ferdinand, was wearing a little pair of dark blue velvet mules.

Corazon Aquino, who succeeded Marcos to the presidency of the Phillipines, put Imelda's shoe collection on public view "so that Filipinos can see how the person who let the populace go hungry indulged herself."

Criticized for her sinful taste for luxury, Imelda defended herself by replying: "It's not true that I owned three thousand pairs of shoes. It was only one thousand and sixty."

Subsequently, Imelda would boast of having come across a sign in a New York shoe shop that read: "There's a little Imelda in all of us."

When she returned to Manila from exile in order to run for the presidency of the republic, she declared on the eve of the elections: "Whether I win or lose, tomorrow I'm still going shopping." She lost.

In 2001, even though her judicial situation had not yet been resolved, Imelda inaugurated a shoe museum in Marikina City, the shoe district of Manila. Many of the shoes on display actually belonged to her, having been retrieved from the presidential palace. On this occasion, too, Imelda was ready with a quick-witted one-liner: "They were looking for skeletons in my cupboard. Instead they only found marvellous objects."

How can you disagree? In *A Dedicated Follower of Fashion*, Holly Brubach writes, "A new pair of shoes cannot mend a broken heart, nor cure a headache. But they can certainly alleviate the symptoms."

Shoe collecting is a phenomenon that spans all ages and geographical barriers. An "Imeldista" will covet shoes no matter the height or shape of heels, colors, or finishes, nor does she discriminate between sneakers and sandals. A true "Imeldista" will desire a fetching model whether it's from a designer's latest collection bought at a boutique, or last year's design from a market stall. An "Imeldista" hoards. Today a pair of pink pumps, tomorrow a sporty ankle boot. We're talking about shoes that might be worn only once because of vagaries in fashion, or shoes bought simply because they were on sale. Shoes that may be too big or too tight but proved irresistible at the moment. When unable to decide between a black pair and a brown pair, the "Imeldista" usually goes for both. Her closets overflow, yet she never has the right shoes to wear with that new dress. So she buys another pair. And maybe yet another, because you never know.

"Imeldistas" are rarely happy people, at least in terms of their shoe collection. Or rather, they're happy in that magic instant of lightheaded folly while actually handing over the money. Love at first sight through the illuminated shop window, followed by lightning physical contact in the shop, which they leave with a healthily flushed countenance. The conquest has been made and pleasure makes the blood throb harder in the veins. And then? And then, just like passion, it's all over. A grubby fingerprint on the upper part of the shoe, a bored glance, regret. "And I thought they looked so good on me. Adieu."

The Point of Life

Listening to women, you'd think they all hated a pointed toe. If this were true, it would be impossible to explain the success of certain shoes that are as sharp as knives. In general, pointed shoes make the feet appear longer and slimmer than they really are. Unfortunately, however, the pointy toe cannot deflect the gaze from other contiguous imperfections: it cannot rescue a footballer's calf nor a less than slender ankle. Indeed, the risk is that it will actually draw attention to these defects, unlike round- or square-toed shoes. And yet . . .

The pointed shoe has the attraction of a forbidden game. This is not a coincidence. Its forebear is the *poulaine,* common in France in the 1400s. It was made of cloth, with a pointed toe that could measure up to three and a half inches long, and was usually covered in pony skin in order to keep the shape intact. In 1486 a papal bull prohibited its use, as it was considered a symbol of indecent vanity.

Little has changed, as the fashion of the last five years does not appear to have come up with anything better than pointy-toed shoes. They give the wearer the illusion of occupying more territory, and consequently of having more power. Teenagers shake off the yoke of childhood the moment they alternate their sneakers with a pair of pointy-toed shoes. A women walking into a meeting of men will use the pointed toe of her shoes to give metaphorical career-orientated kicks to the wearers of classic brogues. She says, "I am here. With these shoes of mine I could actually hurt you. If you don't make some space fore me, I'll carve out some for myself."

The anthropologist Desmond Morris compared the effects of pointy-toed shoes to one of the cruelest forms of physical maiming: the compression of newborn babies' skulls.

This barbarous custom, common among certain primitive cultures of Africa, North and South America, and Europe, alters and inhibits the naturally round growth of the head. The idea is that in adulthood one will appear to be high-born, as a pointed head is incapable of transporting goods, and therefore must be exclusively occupied with noble affairs of the mind. Up until two centuries ago, a few doctors maintained that the shape of the skull had a bearing on the intelligence of the individual.

Similarly, in China, the feet of aristocratic women were bound and prevented from growing; the smaller their feet and the harder it was for them to walk, the more noble, revered, and waited upon they would be.

Thus, our pointy-toed shoes are merely the symbol of a tribe of particularly intelligent women whose skills are wasted on manual work, and who are destined for positions of power.

The Unconscious and the Louis Heel

" **I** don't know who invented high heels, but all men owe him a lot."

Thus spoke Marilyn Monroe, the twentieth century's most marvelous wiggler.

But heels don't just come in high or low. They can also have different, sometimes highly elaborate shapes. Amongst Yves Saint Laurent's latest offering of sandals, there are some with transparent plexiglass heels, a kind of aquarium, inside which are colored or gilded decorations, as well as sequins in motion, and plenty more besides. This is nothing new: already in 1973, there had been Perspex heels and platforms.

The artistic variations of the heel actually originated in the court of Versailles. Louis XIV, the Sun King, was of very short stature, which led him to wear heels. Being the kind of man that he was, he wasn't satisfied with a bit of simple elevation; his heels had to depict miniatures of famous battles or idyllic scenes.

In modern times, the king of heels was Roger Vivier, a French designer who began his career toward the end of the 1930s. From 1953 on, he collaborated with Christian Dior and other famous couturiers.

His signature pieces were bizarrely shaped and decorated heels, almost a form of jewelry worn on the foot. Vivier designed footwear for Marlene Dietrich, Queen Elizabeth (for her wedding day), Josephine Baker, and Catherine Deneuve. Indeed, for the latter, Vivier designed a shoe which was produced by Yves Saint Laurent, and made famous in Luis Buñuel's film *Belle de Jour*: a shoe halfway between a loafer and a pump, decorated with a square metal buckle.

One of his most famous creations, from the early 1960s, consisted of a heel in the shape of a rose thorn, a kind of magnificent miniature sculpture. Today the Vivier brand has been brought back to prominence by Diego Della Valle, who is relaunching it. The new Viviers are designed by Bruno Frisoni, who draws his inspiration from the art of the bygone master but with an added contemporary twist.

For example, a model from his first collection of 2004 is called Madame Psy. While the shape recalls the shoe from *Belle de Jour*, it is decorated with myriad little colored tablets, a kind of ironic tribute to antidepressant pills. In essence, it's a conceptual shoe inviting neurotic women to abandon their Prozac in favor of a new pair of shoes.

One style Roger Vivier worked with extensively was the Louis heel, which has a long story behind it. Launched at the court of Louis XV, it was then shelved for a long time, only to become immensely popular again toward the end of the nineteenth and beginning of the twentieth centuries. For instance, the heels of the boots of the cancan dancers in the Moulin Rouge were Louis heels. At the eve of World War I, in the years when the tango craze was at its peak, women danced in shoes that saw a revival of this coquettish curved heel.

Though it enjoyed mixed fortunes, the Louis heel never disappeared from the scene, without ever having been—at least for many years—the "must have" trend of the season. But there are women who love it a great deal. For two reasons: one practical, the other somewhat less so. The first is that, on the whole, the Louis heel is rarely very high, but thanks to its sinuous lines, it adds a touch of unmistakable femininity. The second is that the Louis heel is a declaration of personality. It has a retro feel, a reasonable compromise between the narrow 1950s "all woman" heel and the clumpy heels worn by their liberated sisters in the late 1960s and early 1970s, as well as saying a great deal about the wearer: "I am a creative individual, an independent woman who has a delightful weakness for beautiful objects."

A "Louis woman" is someone who, on entering a shop, invariably replies to the assistant's query of "How can I help you?" with "I'm looking for something a little bit different." The "Louis woman" has a drawer full of poems, paints watercolors, and plays an instrument. Or at least she'd like to do all of these things. Her unconscious is rich and insinuating, she seeks the nuances in human relationships, and can't for the life of her understand how anyone could be so brazen as to ally herself to current fashion; or, worse still, to be utterly, bravely, out of the fashion loop.

Women in Boots

It is said that it was partly thanks to a pair of boots that Joan of Arc ended up being burned at the stake. The Maid of Orleans, apart from poking her nose into thorny theological questions, was in the habit of wearing a certain kind of footwear, which, in those days (and for some time afterward) was entirely the preserve of men.

Who would hunt, fish, travel, and go to war? Men. Therefore men, and men alone, were allowed to wear boots, while women, responsible for domestic chores, wore little cloth slippers, the luxuriousness of which depended on their social status.

Over the centuries, boots have been the de rigueur footwear for pirates and smugglers. The term "booty" actually derives from the word "boot" and its role as a handy stash for stolen goods. It has even lent its name to music illegally recorded at a concert, still known as "bootleg."

A symbol of virile strength and cunning, boots play a starring role in the classic fairy tale *Puss in Boots,* penned by Charles Perrault, the author of *Cinderella,* who, we all know, held the delicacy of the female foot in high esteem.

Thus, until the mid-nineteenth century, the only boots women were allowed to wear were for riding. After that, however, women other than equestrians and manual laborers were allowed to let their fantasies run wild. In fact, during the Belle Époque, ankle boots with lots of laces became a kind of everyday equivalent of the corset. In Victorian times, short boots were worn to hide the ankle, though in reality, in terms of fashion and morality, they merely exalted it.

It wasn't until recently, in the 1960s, that the female boot was taken to a higher level. Worn with the miniskirt invented by Mary Quant in swinging London, they perfectly epitomized the image of the woman who was freeing herself from all unnecessary frills, as well as sexual and social restraints.

During this period, the idea of a futuristic sex symbol was born out of comic strips and films: The legs of Jane Fonda, playing Barbarella in Roger Vadim's 1968 film of the same name, were sheathed in a pair of mile-high white boots designed for her by the Italian *costumier* Giulio Coltellacci.

Away from the silver screen, out on the streets, women were going for the "space-age" look as interpreted by Courrèges and Paco Rabanne, the stylists to the stars of that period, and their many imitators. Meanwhile, on the radio, Nancy Sinatra's little voice was meowing, "These boots are made for walkin' . . ."

In the early 1970s, two sociological phenomena found a bizarre common ground. The first was a passion for skiing, which was in the process of becoming a sport for the masses, and the second was admiration for the feats of astronauts. Out of these two sparks the Moon Boot was born.

In the following decade, everyone was dancing to "People from Ibiza." In Balearic discos, which give birth to trends that spread to the rest of Europe, even in August, at the height of summer, people were wearing the soft suede boots inspired by the "squaw" style.

But boots have always been connected to the Wild West. You only have to picture cowboy boots and their ilk: footwear for cowboys, resistant to dust but fashionable now in the cities. Just like another western fashion classic: blue jeans.

Finally, we get to the twenty-first century. The "bootography" of the new millennium presents an infinite number of choices. We have different heel heights and calf fittings, and they come in materials to suit every season and any occasion. After a few years in the wilderness, between the mid-1980s and mid-1990s, boots were back, and they're here to stay. There isn't a woman who doesn't own a minimum—and I mean a minimum—of two pairs. You can wear boots with trousers, skirts, with long and short hemlines, by day and by night, at the office and on the weekend.

There are women, perhaps those born with sturdy calves or less-than-perfect ankles, who began to love boots once they understood that in wearing them they could finally wear skirts without feeling uncomfortable. There are women who love short skirts but fear that completely bare legs will create a streetwalker effect. And there are those who simply feel the cold and wear boots because they can no longer bear that icy blade insinuating itself between the hem of one's coat and a pair of shoes that are too scanty for winter. There is that (tiny) minority who have been blessed with a fine pair of knees and know that boots make them appear truly regal. And finally, there are those women (and we're back in Imelda territory here) who immediately understood that, yes, boots are shoes, but on an entirely different plane, and that they are worth collecting even if they do take up rather a lot of space.

Compared to buying a pair of ordinary shoes, the purchase of a pair of boots is a far more complex, and therefore more satisfying, affair. Boots stand out and make their presence felt; they greatly influence the overall look of an outfit. Usually they cost more than a top brand shoe or its equivalent, and therefore the choice has to be carefully weighed. In other words, buying a pair of boots is a strategic purchase, just like a handbag that is designed to be used more or less every day.

Those who are not happy with their calves will leave it to other women to wear those elasticized fabric boots with no zip, as they tend to draw attention to the problem area rather than hide it. Those with thick ankles would do well to choose boots that are cut generously at the top, thus creating a pleasing tapering optical illusion toward the ankle. Women who prefer decorated or unusually colored boots should always pair them up with neutral skirts or outfits, as in this instance the stars are—and should be—the boots.

As long as one bears these caveats in mind, long live the boot, the most formidable footwear for today's modern world. Personally, I would only advise against their use in the following rare instances:

1. Long airline journeys: putting them back on upon arrival is one of the greatest tortures known to woman.
2. Theatrical events by the Italian director Luca Ronconi or films by the Greek director Theo Angelopoulos: after three hours immobile, feet encased in boots can no longer feel a thing.
3. Clandestine amorous assignations: if you get caught *in flagrante,* precious seconds are lost getting dressed.

Ask Me About the Beatles
(Not Those Beatles —
the Ankle Boots)

Beatles are basically a less flashy, more practical variant of knee-high boots. They are mostly worn with trousers, though a few brave souls actually dare to wear them with short skirts. This is a risky business, as the leg gets "cut" at a crucial juncture, and on the whole the look is not kind even to the most well-proportioned types. There is a historical reason for this: the ankle boot was originally created as footwear for men. The first men to be associated with them were the Beatles, whose name became linked to the basic model in black leather with elasticized side panels instead of zips. These are known as "Chelsea boots" by some, "Beatles" by others. Originally the toe was rounded, but eventually it became narrower and more pointed as the prevailing musical culture grew more strident, psychedelic, and transgressive. Further down the line, in the punk and grunge years, the original ankle boot morphed into lace-up Doc Martens, with their armored tank of a sole (inspired by military combat boots) and their *noir* urban feel.

Long before it spawned the Liverpool Four, Britain had contributed to the history of the ankle boot, even a feminine version of it. The famous "Balmorals" worn by Queen Victoria and named after the Scottish royal summer residence were part fabric, part leather. They remained in fashion as long as women wore skirts that reached the ankle, after which they disappeared from sight.

Much later on, when the miniskirt arrived on the scene, the female ankle boot made a comeback, having undergone the same transformation as its "big brother," the knee-high boot. They adapted themselves to the fashion of the day, appearing in unusual materials (plastic, patent leather), or with transparent peepholes along the sides or square toes and metalwork detail. The most imitated model was Courrèges's go-go boot, the highest expression of the taste for space-age fashion.

Devotees of ankle boots are a breed apart, a little like those women who are passionate followers of the Louis heel. The ankle boot reveals a kind of core androgyny in its wearer, which, exceptions apart, indicates a woman who is wedded to her trousers. Usually the collector of ankle boots looks down on the "shoe" shoe, the "skirt" skirt, and the woman who dresses too much like a woman.

The ankle boot hides more of the body than a knee-high and provides a true carapace for the foot, affirming a decisive personality and one untouched by seductive wiles.

A woman in ankle boots, be they sporty or fancy ones, is one who could start a rock band from one day to the next, overturn a board meeting, sell the family firm to set up an agritourism business, and commit other such lunacies. Even more common, the woman in ankle boots is already married or engaged and considers her romantic situation bomb-proof.

However, she would be wise not to count her chickens. Most men like the concept of ankle boots about as much as they like "pop socks"—in other words, not at all! Though they could be swayed, perhaps, by a particularly elegant model, maybe one with eccentric detailing and a feminine heel, which leaves absolutely no ambiguous aftertaste.

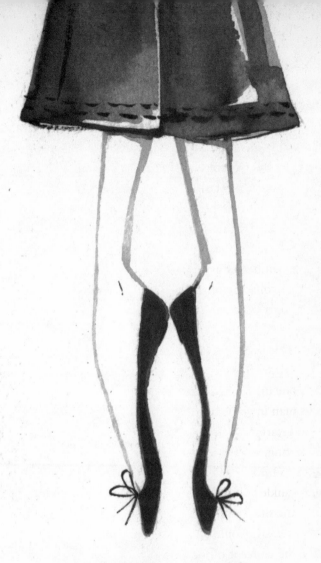

The Ballerina Flat,
and the Eternal Illusion
of Being Audrey

$\mathcal{B}$allerina flats are the shoe equivalent of the white button-down shirt: simple and elegant, they are a classic example of chic that doesn't try too hard. Both the white shirt and flats are inextricably linked to the memory of Audrey Hepburn, a style icon unlike any other.

Audrey was a woman who knew her own mind. Unlike many of today's starlets who entrust themselves to professional stylists, she would choose her outfits in tandem with the couturiers who dressed her (Balenciaga and Givenchy, for example) creating styles alongside them—and sometimes without them.

There is a story told of how one evening, just before an important event, Audrey accidentally spilled coffee on the outfit she was supposed to wear. Picking up any old black skirt, she borrowed one of her husband's white button-down shirts, tied it around her waist, and instantly created a new look.

Similarly, she decided that her height of five feet eight and a half was quite tall enough, and that—to hell with Hollywood stereotypes—she could wear flat shoes without having to compromise one iota of her sex appeal or femininity.

The creator of the shoe that today we call the "flat" was Salvatore Ferragamo, the cobbler born in Irpinia of a large, modest family (he was the eleventh of fourteen children). In the 1920s he became "the man who made shoes for Hollywood." He created footwear for several films, among them *The Ten Commandments* and *The Thief of Bagdad* with Douglas Fairbanks Jr., and was a friend of Rudolf Valentino, Greta Garbo, and Mary Pickford. In the 1930s, he returned to Italy and established himself in Florence, where stars and celebrities from all walks of life continued to visit him.

For years, Ferragamo dressed the feet of Queen Elizabeth, the duke and duchess of Windsor, Queen Maria José of Italy, Italian actresses such as Sophia Loren and Anna Magnani, and international celebrities such as Carmen Miranda, Marilyn Monroe, and Ingrid Bergman. Ferragamo products were—and still are—considered to be the felicitous result of the squaring of the circle; elegant, original shoes that are always extremely comfortable to wear.

Naturally, when Audrey Hepburn arrived in Italy to shoot *Roman Holiday*, she turned to Salvatore for her shoes and remained an affectionate client of his until her death.

As a young girl she had studied dance, and her ballerina's posture was one component of her natural beauty. It is also how the idea of the ballerina flat came to Ferragamo. The patent for this shoe was not deposited at the State Central Archives until 1957, but the product had already been manufactured for at least three years. In the original drawing, preserved at the Ferragamo Museum, you can see perfectly how the designer transformed a real ballet shoe into an everyday walking "flat."

Still using Audrey as his muse, Ferragamo also created other versions of the flat, one of which was in essence a low-cut shoe with a very low and graceful heel. From then on it has been called the "Sabrina heel" after the unforgettable film of the same name in which the actress starred.

Now, as we haven't all been born as tall and genetically blessed as Audrey Hepburn, choosing the ballerina flat, depending on your viewpoint, can be seen as an act either of extreme courage or extreme arrogance.

There are two categories of flat-wearers. The first consists of little queens of understatement impervious to the clamorous demands of fashion—particularly beautiful and well-proportioned creatures who wear these shoes with nonchalance. Knowing that they have no need to, they do not wear makeup, and only the same few pieces of jewelry. To these perfect, Audrey-like creatures, one can say nothing.

However, there is also a second category who see flats as aspirational objects; by wearing them, these poor deluded creatures think they will become as chic as Audrey. Sorry to disappoint, but it's not that easy. If there is one shoe in the world that demands fine ankles, and above all a perfect foot and impeccable bearing, it is the flat. In most models, the arch of the foot is neither lifted nor supported; and there is the risk of slopping around as though one were wearing slippers. In other words, flats are very lovely, but not terribly helpful. And yet, it is unusual to find a woman who doesn't own at least one pair. In fact, many would call them their favorite shoes, the ones they wear day in and day out, and which, once they are worn out, are replaced by an almost identical pair.

Some men like flats. These are mostly short types who don't like being overshadowed by an overly imposing companion. The story of Tom Cruise, ex-husband of the beanpole Nicole Kidman, is a universal one. Upon their divorce, Nicole let the newspapers know that she now had at least one reason to be happy: she could finally wear heels.

However, most men just don't like flats. They sulk when we want to watch *Breakfast at Tiffany's* for the hundredth time to rejoice in Audrey's elegance. They tell us that women like Audrey as a style icon, but that she wasn't the least bit sexy. These are men who think that sexiness all comes down to the height of your heels. Men who never noticed Brigitte Bardot's appearance on this planet. She was another great flat-wearer, but one who interpreted them in her own way, and in doing so became the walking symbol of a wild, free sensuality.

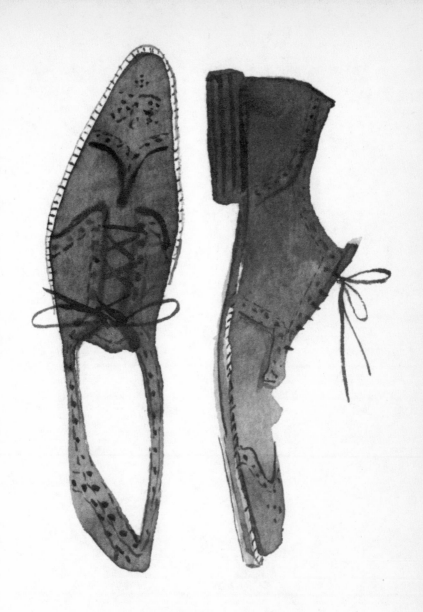

The Other Hepburn,
and Men's Shoes

Katharine Hepburn was born of a suffragette mother and a doctor father. As a young girl, she was reared in the cult of modernity and independence. Thus, even though she chose to enter the superficial world of bright lights and illusion in Hollywood, Katharine interpreted the role of diva, and the star system, in her own unique way. She loathed skirts, above all because they obliged her to wear garter belts, and therefore she almost always wore trousers. Who knows, if she had been born in the era of panty hose sans garter belts, she might never have created the extraordinary, much copied, androgynous style that made her famous. Her wide trousers perfectly matched the men's shoes that she had made to measure.

The first famous woman to choose men's shoes and make them fashionable in the 1920s was Eleanor Roosevelt (1884–1962), the niece of the American president, Theodore. Wife of another president, Franklin Delano, who was also a distant cousin, Eleanor often wore a kind of clunky lace-up shoe known as the "oxford," chosen for practicality rather than fashion. The First Lady did a great deal for the female cause; she offered herself up as a strong-minded leader and represented an entire generation of women who, having grown up between two world wars and the Depression, were divorced from useless frivolities. Female fashion had already begun to change during World War I: skirts were shorter and looser and made from robust but cheaper materials. But the most important change was the disappearance of the corset, an atrocious instrument of torture reserved for the female sex. One of the slogans printed on American government leaflets at the time was Loose Hips Build Ships. With more on their minds than fashion, the wives, mothers, and girlfriends of men at war could not have worn anything but low, comfortable shoes suitable for riding a bicycle, going out to work, procuring rationed food, and, in Europe, running from bombs. In those days, women were soldiers in civvies.

Pretty soon, the androgynous style of certain shoes, beneath the glamorous lights of cinema, began to acquire other, less severe, qualities. Worn by stars such as the eccentric, mysterious, and possibly gay Greta Garbo, lace-up shoes acquired a touch of ambiguity. On the feet of another diva, Marlene Dietrich, they even launched a new look of elegance and sex appeal. The German actress and singer was a passionate expert on shoes, who once said, "Shoes are much more important than frocks or suits. They give elegance to an entire look. My advice is to buy one pair of excellent quality shoes, as opposed to three cheap pairs, or ones that you're not entirely sure of."

Of the two hundred pairs of shoes Dietrich owned, there were many lace-up, two-toned models known in the trade as "spectators." They were originally created as walking shoes for wealthy men, to be worn exclusively in warm weather. They were often made of cream-colored fabric, with only the point, the heel, and the middle in leather.

Marlene adopted them at once, wearing them under her beloved trouser suits. Around the same period, Coco Chanel was inspired by the same two-tone motif to create her own cult shoe, a classic that has never become dated: a cream-colored upper, with a black rounded toe in either leather or patent leather.

Mademoiselle Chanel admitted to having designed those shoes in order to make her own feet, which she found too large, appear smaller. She was right; the optical illusion never fails.

While we're on the subject of optical illusions, remember: if you wear light-colored shoes, never wear dark hose, and vice versa. This lesson comes once again courtesy of Marlene Dietrich. Whether in a skirt or trousers, the Blue Angel never wore stockings that contrasted with her shoes. The uniform coloring of shoe and stocking has the instantaneous effect of lengthening the leg. We, girls of the new millennium, should take heed of Marlene's rule because, let's face it, she was someone who knew a thing or two about legs.

A Brief Course in Self-Esteem
(Regarding the Length
of a Shoe Strap)

A shoe with a strap, in footwear terms, is what Vladimir Nabokov's *Lolita* is to the male fantasy: naive in appearance, perverse in substance. The basic design of this type of shoe (which comprises a round or square toe, and a fairly low strap in relation to the arch) is known as a Mary Jane. The name derives from a kind of children's shoe worn by Mary Jane, the little sister of Buster Brown, a character created to advertise shoes in the early twentieth century. As with many other shoe styles, this one's most famous ambassador was an actress, a baby diva by the name of Shirley Temple.

Since then the Mary Jane has experienced a tremendous evolution. There are versions that call to mind the actual children's shoes, while others have a medium-high heel, like a "Louis," which recalls the dance shoes of the twenties. Finally, there are models where the base has been widened and the toe enlarged into a kind of gigantic cookie shape, like Campers. Recently the designer Marc Jacobs used Mary Janes in referential terms to exalt childhood in cartoon form. But this is not the point; the point is that Mary Janes are, par excellence, the shoe with a strap. Straps, which can be found on very high sandals, on stiletto court shoes, on reinterpreted flats, are a lethal detail. They can destroy even the most beautiful legs or the finest ankles. They heighten skinniness or create the illusion of chubbiness. They can even make the skirt above them appear ugly. I say skirt, because while some people do wear strap shoes with trousers, it nevertheless remains a cowardly, turncoat act.

Thus, to wear this kind of shoe, you need to have a highly developed sense of self-esteem. They're for very confident women who believe utterly in their own worth regardless of the shoes they're wearing. In other words, these women are an endangered species indeed—heroic pandas of femininity.

Oh, and another small detail, there's the problem of fastening the bloody strap. The buckle always comes loose, the little hole you stick the pin in is never where you want it to be, and you often end up having to fasten it any old way, only to discover not long after that it has come loose. Besides which, classic Mary Janes don't even have buckles on the end of the straps but instead have buttons, which are often coated in slippery varnish—a diabolical invention that breaks nails and invites malediction. This is why a pair of Mary Janes, in spite of never having been worn much for all of the above-mentioned reasons, end up being put out to pasture earlier than other shoes because the strap has broken and the shoemaker implacably decrees that there's nothing to be done. Thus, the Mary Jane is the most insidious of shoes, just as Lolita is the most insidious of women.

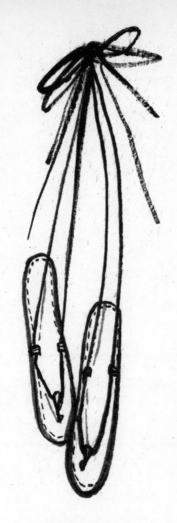

Sandal,

Your Name Is Scandal

$\mathcal{S}$andals, which evolved from the simple need to put *something* on one's feet, were the footwear of choice for all primitive peoples. There isn't an ancient civilization that didn't try to perfect them; from Africa to India, China to the Mediterranean, they are what our forebears wore. Barefoot, but not too barefoot. Anthropologically speaking, sandals are the Darwinian missing link between *Homo sapiens* and the *Female heel-totterer* of today.

The ancients wore many of the same designs that we love now. The thong flip-flop, which these days is ubiquitous (albeit in a luxurious version), in cities, has many precedents, an example being the ceremonial *geta* clogs that Japanese girls wear during certain religious rites to signal their transition to adulthood. Scandalous sandals are even mentioned in the Bible: just before being beheaded by Judith, Holofernes had stopped to admire her fabulous sandals. Poor Holofernes, an *ante litteram* fetishist who was cruelly punished for his weakness.

In ancient times, the sandal was democratic footwear, worn by both slaves and gladiators, noblemen and concubines, in marketplaces and imperial courts from Rome to Persia. The differences lay in the materials. Papyrus and straw for the bricklayers working on the pyramids, spun gold studded with gems for the Cleopatras, Messalinas, and Agrippinas of the day. Pagan rituals showed an appreciation of sandals: there are statues of Aphrodite, naked apart from a pair of sensual thongs on her feet, and of Minerva wearing extremely elegant masculine gladiator sandals to match her female warrior's outfit. Naturally, Christianity and the Middle Ages did away with all that nudity and for many centuries in the West, at least, the erotic sandal slipped into obscurity. The further society advanced, the less keen it became on the *sauvage* idea of the naked foot, which came to be regarded as a symbol of either poverty or barbarism.

The triumphant rehabilitation of the sandal is a relatively recent phenomenon. Its rediscovery occurred in the last century and was tied to the concept of the holiday or vacation, a relaxed time during which wealthy men and women were finally granted the voluptuous pleasure of sporting a seminaked foot. A genius among sandalmakers was André Perugia, an Italo-Frenchman born in Nice at the end of the nineteenth century who, in the late 1920s, became the trusted designer of the French couturier Paul Poiret. Inspired by the temperate climate of the Côte d'Azur, and the ladies who took their holidays there, Perugia launched the fashion of summer sandals. His first clients were so-called "fallen" women, actresses and showgirls, among them the sex symbols of the day such as Mistinguett and Josephine Baker.

The 1940s and 1950s saw the invention of a middle way: moderately low-cut sandals with the front part of the foot covered save for a little window that exposed the toes—a voyeur's peephole. This peep toe, however, was merely the beginning. The actress Shelley Winters once said how often she and Marilyn Monroe would steal shoes from the studio wardrobes. A heist she was particularly proud of involved a pair of elaborate sandals with ankle straps, high heels, and a great big bow on the toes, which the two giggling thieves nicknamed "Fuck Me Shoes."

Nowadays, not only is full-foot nudity permissible, but the

range of sandals available has become as varied as that of ordinary closed-toe shoes. You can now get high-heeled sandals and flat sandals, colored ones and transparent ones, strappy sandals and strapless ones, daytime sandals and evening sandals, city sandals and leisure sandals. The great designer André Pfuster created the Deauville, with its open basket-weave upper, widely imitated in every possible color and material.

Every summer the purveyors of sexy shoes come up with a wealth of new designs for sandals. A model that undoubtedly would have appealed to Shelley Winters is René Caovilla's "Serpent": it displays a naked foot with no upper or straps whatsoever, a perilously high heel, and only a spiral of crystals to support the ankle. Incredibly, it is actually possible to walk in these shoes—at least for some women.

While the "sandalist" explosion might have brought into prominence the "fuck me shoe," a downside has been the liberalization and diffusion of what is undoubtedly one of the most comfortable, yet ugliest, shoes known to man: the Birkenstock, a flat, broad sandal hitherto associated with the image of the German tourist. Originally created in Germany in 1967 in one of those mysterious quirks of fashion, they soon became de rigueur in the hotbed radical campuses of San Francisco. Worn by hippies, beatniks, and flower children, they were seen as a groundbreaking and unisex symbol of freedom, both for the brain and the foot. As far as women were concerned, they were worn like a badge proclaiming that intellectual girls did not want to be considered objects. Thus, as we're far enough removed today to finally admit it, one of the casualties of bra burning and that grim war between the sexes was a sense of aesthetics.

It's no coincidence that Birkenstocks failed to take root in Italy. In fact, for years, regardless of political persuasion, we would look on with horror as every summer foreigners' feet shod in Birkenstocks traipsed through our artistic cities. Up above you would see Giotto's bell tower, or Raphael's Madonna—down below, a Birkenstock stuffed with a white ankle sock. *Horribile visu!*, as the ancient Romans would have said. How is it possible to immerse oneself in such a harmony of colors and proportions, and yet remain oblivious to one's own feet?

Today, however, I am forced to admit the truth: Birkenstocks, and their ugly cousins, Dr. Scholl's clogs, have won. Not only have they been given the aesthetic green light, but they have actually been taken up by trendy designers such as Marc Jacobs as a kind of fashion archetype to be reinvented and elaborated upon. Patrick Cox, designer of the unisex "Wannabe" in the 1990s, called Birkenstocks "modern and comfortable, a perennial classic." Glad to hear it!

Luckily, shoe history, like all history, has its highways and by-ways, so one hopes that this aberrant fashion will soon have had its day.

In the meantime, another dangerous fashion is lurking in the wings: the return of the sandal-inspired footwear of the ancient world riding on the wave of recent films such as *Gladiator* and *Troy*. This sandal is a catastrophe in every sense. The foot is left almost revoltingly bare and the tie-up version, with leather thongs crisscrossing to the knee, requires one to be a perfect physical specimen in order to wear it.

Even when the design is less revealing and more flattering, the sandal remains a beautiful and yet tricky object, at times a mission impossible. Unlike all other shoes, whose main function is to cover the foot, the sandal lays it bare—the bikini of footwear. There's no point in wearing the most beautiful and precious sandals in the world if you have to expose a pair of feet that would be better left covered.

Thus, as summer approaches, even those women most resistant to beauty treatments cave in to the ritual of the pedicure, to polish that beautifies the toenails, and so forth. The sensual freedom afforded by wearing sandals makes all the patience required for hours under a nail dryer worthwhile. On the other hand, you could take a leaf out of the book of one of my girlfriends, a super-organized and supersophisticated creature from Mantua who—come rain or shine—carries a pair of flip-flops around in her bag. She parks her car outside the beauty salon and when she's done, she dries her nail polish with the car heater as she's driving home.

The Law of the Heel

Instinctively, I feel like saying: Girls, boycott mules! They're tricky, unreliable shoes. For a start, it's hard to buy them in the right size. In the shop, your foot slides a bit forward and a bit backward and it's never quite clear if they're a comfortable fit. Take it from me, mules are not comfortable shoes.

Mules are not made for walking. They are shoes born of centuries of indoor living in the houses of the rich and the powerful, reaching their apex in the mid-seventeenth century. Even then, the mule was more a frivolous accessory than a real shoe—an *objet* of skilled craftsmanship created to showcase embroidery, precious fabrics such as velvet and brocade, gems, and other decorative gewgaws. Mules were the caprice of kings, queens, and courtesans who stayed inside the palace or traveled around in a carriage.

Mules were born flat, then were raised up on heels, but it was on the uppers that the master slipper makers really let their imaginations run riot. Basically, the little slipper that evolved into what we call a mule today was a bit like a tapestry. Now tell me, today, what would you do with a tapestry? Nothing. Because how, with our tapestry mules, are we supposed to get around, especially in cities such as Rome or Florence where irregular cobblestones are just waiting to send us flying?

It must also be said that any shoes that leave the heel exposed are never comfortable. And this includes any number of bare-heel situations: perched atop a mule or a classy sandal, or even inside a pair of Dutch clogs, a 1970s fashion that has had its day. It seems impossible, yet thanks to the iniquitous demands of fashion there were women who willingly chose to suffer in clogs. The victims of ankle sprains during the feminist rallies of the 1970s remain too numerous to be counted.

In mules, the heel searches in vain for a permanent center of gravity. Furthermore, let's get things straight—the heel is not a beautiful thing to behold. All men think so, though few admit it; for them, the sexy part of the foot is the toes. It's difficult to believe that in Victorian times the heel was considered obscene, the equivalent of the female bottom. Crazy. Today's woman's heels are often a little on the ugly side, and dry and white if not looked after properly. Faced with the sight of a heel, the male libido plummets, just as when faced with a pair of teddy-bear-patterned pajamas.

The only instance, apart from at the beach, in which the sight of a heel is acceptable, is the Chanel sling-back: closed at the toe, open at the back, but with a strap around the heel.

Here too the ingenious Coco had a revolutionary insight. Women like the idea of mules, she thought, but as flapping shoes are not an attractive look, she found a way of securing the wandering foot with a strap that supports the back of the ankle and confers stability and decency in one stroke.

Unfortunately, as is the case of many of Chanel's inventions, the "sling-back" has achieved such classic status that it has become almost boring. And yet there are situations where it is worth considering; for example, going to the office in the summer, or to a spring wedding. Or when the décolletage of a sandal is too much, a Chanel shoe, perhaps in a slightly unusual color, is simply perfect.

Take to Your Platforms!

In the third act of *Hamlet*, the Prince of Denmark lays into poor Ophelia for being too vain. He thunders: "I have heard of your paintings too, well enough; God has given you one face, and you make yourselves another. You jig, you amble . . . and make your wantonness your ignorance."

According to Shakespeare scholars and British fashion historians, "you jig, you amble" is a reference to none other than *chopines*, the towering stacked shoes that were the fashion of the day. Much more than shoes, these were veritable pedestals that could reach as high as twenty inches tall, upon which ladies would be placed by the sturdy arms of their maidservants. The fashion of chopines originated in Venice, first among prostitutes, then among respectable ladies. According to some sources, they came over from Turkey, where the stiltlike shoes were used in the baths to keep the feet aboveground and dry. Others say they came from Spain, where there was an abundance of cork, a light material ideally suited to stilts.

Whatever its origins, this Venetian fashion spread all over Europe, and Elizabeth I of England was one of its followers. Hamlet's outburst was therefore also a jab at the sovereign, who owned a collection of chopines.

The chopines craze was as brief as it was excessive; by the early 1600s, women had climbed down from their stilts, and there they would remain . . . until, just before World War II, in Florence, when Salvatore Ferragamo showed the prototype of his first "platforms" to one of his clients, Duchess Visconti di Modrone. The appalled noblewoman declared, "Salvatore, these shoes are an abomination! What *were* you thinking of?" To which Ferragamo replied, "Duchess, I ask you for a small favor. Wear these shoes tomorrow to Sunday mass; if even one of your friends compliments you on them, I'll make you a pair of shoes of your own design for free."

That Sunday, in church, the ladies of Florence only had eyes and words for the duchess's shoes. And thus, platforms came to rule the entire 1940s. They turned out to be practical and economical, innovative in their shape and design. Ferragamo, and other designers after him, created diverse decorative patterns. The "stilts" principle shifted over to sandals, closed shoes, day footwear, and evening footwear.

However, after the war, the curtain fell on platform shoes; they were too reminiscent of the years of economic isolation and misery. For women, too, they were in love at first sight with the fresh stiletto heels that were such an ideal accompaniment to the new look proposed by Christian Dior.

Platforms would make their comeback in the early 1970s, under the bright lights of glam rock. Bisexuality, eccentricity, excess, and sequins accompanied the music of the day. Its poster boys were the English stars Elton John, David Bowie, and T. Rex's Marc Bolan, who were all photographed wearing brightly colored boots and shoes with impossibly high platforms—sometimes reaching as high as six or seven inches. Street fashion followed suit: the dominant look consisted of fitted jackets, tight—very tight—trousers that clung to the sexual organs, and bell bottoms that flowed out over the gigantic platform shoes.

It was an era of "glittering" fashion, so over the top as to appear decadent—but almost as quickly as it began, the revolutionary flame that had blazed a decade earlier in swinging London was guttering. By 1977, the working-class dancer John Travolta (Tony Manero in *Saturday Night Fever*) had lowered his platforms by several inches. From then on, the male platform shoe virtually disappeared, making an appearance only as an oddity in transsexual shows, a kind of parody of femininity.

However, for women, the platform shoe continues to wax and wane according to the vagaries of fashion. The Spice Girls brought them back in for a couple of seasons; and every now and then they reappear, but by and large they remain embarrassing fashion objects (perhaps thanks to their saucy origins among the prostitutes of Venice), which you either love or hate.

Platforms are popular among women who want to appear taller but can't abide traditional narrow high heels. Eccentrics also like them because, if well designed, the shoe is transformed into a kind of sculptured pedestal.

Yet at the same time there exists an entirely different category of woman who will not even hear them mentioned. Platforms, be they low or high ones, are perceived as vulgar, showy, and crass. But when we denigrate platforms, we are unwittingly slipping into Hamlet mode—a poetic moralist who was also a royal pain, and unqualified in matters of fashion.

In truth, platform shoes, particularly in the pure style of the 1940s, can be extremely elegant, provided they are worn with an appropriate outfit. For example, they look wonderful with a flowery silk frock that flows down to the knee, but are an abomination matched with a tight-fitting pencil skirt. Platforms with miniskirts are strictly forbidden, also with cigarette pants, or, worse still, pedal pushers.

On the other hand, if you wear platform sandals under a pair of trousers in an elegant fabric, worn long enough to skim the upper of the shoe, you'll walk like a queen. I happened to meet Monica Bellucci dressed like this, and never did a pair of platforms appear so elegant.

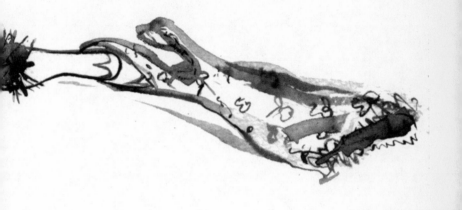

Globalization and the Crisis
in the Western Slipper

While we're all capable of looking elegant in a pair of evening sandals or shoes, it's trickier trying to maintain a certain dignity in slippers. Just the name itself is a downer. And to think that in distant times, the slipper was an object of luxury, indeed a status symbol: as a mark of respect, one would kiss those of popes, bishops, and cardinals! Instead, nowadays, a *pantofolaio* (slipper-wearer, or couch potato) is a sullen, enervated creature lacking in vitality and interests apart from his remote control and television, which he can use quite easily regardless of what horrors he's wearing on his feet.

This is why, in twenty-first-century households, slippers are either exhibits from a horror museum or, in the best-case scenario, exotic souvenirs.

If you want to learn more about your ever-mysterious neighbors, go and knock on their doors around suppertime with an innocuous request for an onion or a pinch of salt. This way, you'll catch them unawares, and by seeing what they wear on their feet in those moments when their sense of decorum lowers its guard, you will finally get to find out who you're really sharing your apartment building with.

There are fathers of daddy's girls who, in order to make their little darlings happy, walk around the house with two gigantic furry Disney ducks on their feet; and mothers of spoiled, PlayStation-addicted sons who please them by wearing Chip the chipmunk on one foot and Dale on the other. There are fifty-year-old women who in public boast of their journeys to the Orient; only during a bit of late-night TV viewing in the presence of Gigi Marzullo do they dare to wear a certain pair of extremely pointed Moroccan slippers with a lingering smell of goat that has not faded since the summer of 1985. Then there's a flock of chilly ladies and young women who, even in Naples, either opt for colored *friuliane* velvet slippers (until recently, found only in Venice); or else skid around the floor in thick boiled-wool socks embroidered with edelweiss, which they bought at Cortina d'Ampezzo.

At supper, in the most unlikely Italian households, amazing things will appear: slippers fit for a Turkish grand vizier ("I got them at the market in Istanbul for a song"), little Chinese slippers as modeled by the Gang of Four (in these cases, usually the entire family democratically opts to wear them), and splendid crimson velvet Burmese thongs so beautiful that it's almost a waste to wear them indoors, considering what a statement they'd make out on the street.

Thus, the modern slipper is as robustly multiethnic as the world we live in. Nothing wrong with that—we're globally content about it. But certain, crucial questions remain, which we hope may be answered in the future.

First, what became of the dignified, slightly sad-looking smooth leather slippers our parents and grandparents used to wear? I would imagine that the bulk of them are now destined for places like Turkey, China, or Burma while we amuse ourselves with those nations' offerings, but I can't be certain of this.

A second question: What happened to *pattine*? These little cloth squares worn beneath shoes were at the height of their popularity in the early 1960s, coinciding with a boom in electric floor polishers. All European mothers insisted that they be worn, and "I don't want marks on my floor" was the shriek that would greet one upon entering the house. Today, adieu *pattine,* adieu mother's housewifely little foibles, and adieu to those floors that resembled the skating rink for Holiday on Ice.

A third and final question: What happened to those ladies' slippers with a little heel and a tuft of pink marabou feathers on the front? Marilyn Monroe wore them in the 1955 film *The Seven Year Itch*. Kitschy and sublime, they were, and I saw one of the last remaining pairs in the flesh in Moda Stile, a dusty old-fashioned shop in Verona. I considered buying a pair as a souvenir from a bygone era. I'm sorry now that I didn't, as the shop is no longer there; it's become a jeans outlet.

Rain: A Divine Punishment

I_n the $winter$ of 1985, there was an immense snowfall in northern Italy that lasted several days. News reports of the day testified to an interesting escalation in footwear designed to protect oneself from what one journalist called "the white visitor." Day one: optimism, normal shoes. Day two: heavier shoes with reinforced rubber soles. Day three: fur-lined boots. Day four onward: Moon Boots for après-ski became the order of the day, and indeed some people were spotted wearing high-top fishing boots on the Underground, the only transport system left running in Milan during that period.

This episode illustrates how remaining elegant in the snow or rain is a virtual impossibility. Furthermore, it might even be said that inclement weather rains down from the sky in order to castigate female vanity.

This is extremely well demonstrated in a fairy tale by Hans Christian Andersen, who was originally a cobbler by trade: "The Girl Who Trod on the Loaf." The author of "The Red Shoes," another tale in which shoes bring nothing good, outdoes himself this time in terms of dark morality.

Inger, the heroine of "The Girl Who Trod on the Loaf," is a pretty and flirtatious little maid who owns a pair of delectable new shoes. Inger's kind mistress persuades her to bring some bread to the poor old mother she has left behind in her village. Inger, wickedly, has no intention of going to visit her mother because she is ashamed of her. The only reason she agrees to her mistress's request is that it will give her the opportunity to preen in front of her ex-neighbors. On the way, in order not to dirty her shoes, she throws the loaf down into the mud so that she can cross a marsh, but as punishment her feet stick to the loaf and she sinks down into the marsh. Her feet are stuck in her shoes (the fate also of the unlucky heroine of "The Red Shoes") and the loaf is stuck to the shoes, thus condemning Inger to starve unto eternity.

It must have been in order to avoid a similar end that vain New Yorkers, during the particularly harsh winter of 2003–2004 (18 degrees below zero) took to wearing the Australian boots called UGGs. They became an instant cult, once they were photographed on the feet of women like Kate Moss, Madonna, and Demi Moore. They are so warm, you can wear them without socks, even in a snowstorm.

This is as may be, but the truth is that we women are usually put on the spot even by a common garden-variety downpour. I have a friend, an extremely elegant antiquarian, who admits she can't bring herself to buy any kind of "walking shoe," especially the kind designed for unknown terrain and bad weather.

It matters little if Burberry, the brand of the famous raincoats, has come up with Wellington boots in their trademark tartan, or that you can also buy Chanel Wellingtons. At the end of the day, they're still Wellies, shapeless rubber objects suited to guerrillas, or members of the Home Guard, in bad weather.

It's no coincidence that the term *galoshes* derives from the Gauls; once the Romans had conquered them, they stole from them the idea of covering their boots with leather strips to protect against the rain.

These primitive galoshes were in essence a kind of overshoe, similar to those worn in the nineteenth century. Andersen also devoted a story, "The Galoshes of Fortune," to this kind of footwear; but unlike "The Red Shoes" and "The Girl Who Trod on the

Loaf," here he deals with their positive, magical virtues. The overshoes, gift of a fairy, have the power to instantly transport the wearer to any place and epoch of their choice—space and time being no obstacle.

Who knows, maybe they're due for a comeback.

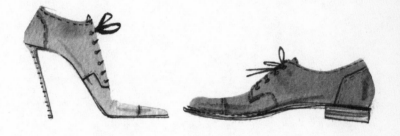

What Men Say When They Talk About Shoes

We know that women commit several errors when they fall in love. One of these is not paying attention to men's shoes. We're so wrapped up in what's on our own feet that we scarcely give a second glance to theirs. For example, is it possible to fall in love with a man wearing diarrhea-colored woven leather loafers? No, it's not, and yet let me assure you, it happens. Not just because love is blind, but because we women are so ignorant about men's shoes.

Usually when a woman accidentally strays into the men's department of a shoe shop, she yawns, then beats a hasty retreat. Bad, very bad. Girls in search of either a husband or just companionship would do well to become experts in the field, because a sizable number of men might find this irresistibly appealing.

Men are mostly pretty well informed about what's on their feet, without necessarily going to the lengths of the actor Daniel Day Lewis, who, during a sabbatical year from acting, apprenticed himself to a Florentine shoemaker in order to learn how to make shoes.

So what do men make of a woman who can help them choose a pair of shoes? Pretty much the same as what they make of a woman who understands the offsides rule: that she's the bee's knees. Naturally, being men, they don't want a woman to be actually better informed than they, as that would be dangerous. Still, it's worth knowing the basic differences between types of shoes; whatever happens, it's a great opening gambit, and in the best-case scenario you might actually find yourself helping him choose shoes for his, and indeed *your,* wedding.

Should you be successful, it is worth bearing in mind a few fundamental differences between male and female shoe lovers. Men brush and polish their shoes with loving care, while it is a well-known fact that we find this chore to be insufferably boring. Men appreciate shoes that last, while women prefer continually changing theirs. Finally, unlike women who choose shoes on a whim, men always have a clear idea as to which shoes suit any given occasion: lace-ups for the office, black for special occasions, loafers for leisure time, heavy ankle boots for inclement weather, Docksiders for sailing, and so forth—all highly practical, and, from where we're standing, utterly devoid of all imagination. Which is how it should be. Guys—leave the over-the-top stuff to us!

However, cohabitation between shoe lovers of differing sexes is possible. In order to get the ball rolling, it is helpful for women to be *au fait* with the basic rules of the world of men's shoes. Dear reader, stay with me at this point and try not to yawn. Here follow five opening gambits to leave your male interlocutor open-mouthed with astonishment.

- Men's shoes began to differentiate themselves from women's toward the end of the fifteenth century, rumored to be thanks to a physical defect of Charles VIII of France. The king, who reigned from 1493 to 1498, had six toes on each foot and as a result would commission particularly wide-toed, square shoes to be made for him. This fashion spread across all of Europe, arriving in England, where Henry VIII and his court began wearing shoes whose soles were six and a half inches wide: the wider the sole, the richer and more powerful you appeared to be.

- The eighteenth century saw the fashion of gigantic buckles; the nineteenth favored romantic decoration. The turning point for the modern male shoe came toward the end of the nineteenth century. Europe began to import American models, which, with continual modifications, bring us to the present day. The main ones are Bostons or oxfords (lace-ups), bulldogs (a half boot with a buttoned flap in the front), and derbys (two-tone oxfords). Even loafers come from the United States, originally part of the "preppie" look worn by nice boys graduating from preparatory schools.

- High boots, worn throughout the ages, saw their popularity plummet after World War II. They were considered too closely associated with the image of Nazism and fascism, though who knows, maybe at some point their moment will return.

- The pointed male shoe, fashionable in Edwardian times, made a neo-dandy comeback with the advent of the Teddy Boys, young men who rejected their fathers' shabby suits in favor of elegant Edwardian suits.

- Desert boots, the leisure footwear of the 1950s, are merely a more sophisticated version of the boots worn by General Montgomery's Eighth Army in Egypt.

The Mysterious Magic
of Red Shoes

There is an Anglo-Saxon proverb: "Red and Yellow / To catch a fellow." Nowadays, unless you've set your sights on a Roma or Lecce football fan (red and yellow being the colors of both the above-mentioned clubs), I doubt whether pairing up these two garish colors would lead to any particularly interesting results.

That said, red shoes, and only red shoes, merit a chapter of their own. In fact, they even merit a little poem. (Oh, all right then, a rhyme.) Here it is:

On display in the window of a shop,
A red shoe, you'll find, is always top;
Low heeled, or high heeled, with a buckle, or without
The red shoe's the one that always stands out.

The others are all brown, or maroon, or black;
Fun is what those colors lack,
While a red shoe is wild and full of high jinks
Turning each woman into a playful minx.

A red shoe brings endless good fortune
That can even reach to the moon;
A red shoe is a charm,
That will keep you from harm.

"They're *so* last season, I'm chucking mine"
Say the know-all girls—we know their kind;
But don't listen to them, just follow your heart
Give your feet wings—from your red shoes don't part.

And when your aunt says they're not respectable,
That in such a color you'll be a spectacle:
You calmly reply, "I couldn't give a damn,
I intend to have as many as I can."

Wearing red shoes will give your day wings,
Energy, pizzazz, and other such things!
Put them on and a witch you'll become
Sexy and powerful, all rolled into one.

Trade Secrets
and Other Devilments

Heel Heights

The most popular heel height in production is between two and three inches, known in shoemaking jargon as between 50 and 70 points.

A higher heel is three and a half inches tall, though on some occasions it can even be four inches.

Shoes used on the catwalk can go up to four and three-quarters inches tall, but they are almost always lowered to four inches before reaching the street.

A heel under two inches can have several variations: a pump can range from flat to half an inch, while a loafer is around one inch.

Short women tend to go for high heels, while those taller than five feet six inches often suffer from the same syndrome that befell Nicole Kidman when she was married to the vertically challenged Tom Cruise—i.e., trying not to tower over him.

In truth, there are no hard and fast rules. Just lots of women of different heights and with different viewpoints. There are short and tall women who would quite happily climb mountains in three-and-a-half-inch heels and actually feel uncomfortable wearing sneakers, which half the world consider to be the *ne plus ultra* of comfort.

On the other hand, certain women don't like heels but still wear them, either because it's the thing to do, or because they think they look better in them. You can recognize these women as they totter along looking worried and suffering. They have the look of those kids who yesterday were dressed in jeans and sweatshirts, and today have donned a suit and tie to present their university thesis.

It's impossible to be either attractive or elegant if you feel and look awkward. Thus, everyone needs to find the heel that suits them, as every height commands its own posture; what one person finds comfortable might not be so for another.

To avoid rash purchases, next time take a ruler and measure the heel height of the shoes you wear most. There's nothing wrong with wearing the same kind of heel; in fact, you avoid having to take up and let down your trousers ad nauseam; once and for all you establish your manner of walking or, in a nutshell, your style.

Not only that, a consistent deportment will avoid that annoying question that always makes us feel like frauds: "How come you look so tall today? Are you wearing heels?"

Perfect Maintenance

"A good cleaning lengthens the life of your shoe, which is now a question of national importance. Your shoes will last longer if you paid a decent amount for them, and if you keep them well-polished and soled, and in a state of good repair." These pearls of wisdom appeared in an edition of English *Vogue* from June 1941: the war was on, money was tight, and a great respect abounded for the nation's most popular means of transport.

Nowadays, caring for your shoes is not only a good way of saving money, it is also a way of showing love toward these uniquely special objects. Besides which, a woman can be dressed to the nines, but dusty shoes or worn-out heels are as bad as chipped nail polish or, worse still, stockings with runs. So, grab some shoe polish and let's see some elbow grease.

- Use only suitable products; never be tempted to make your own concoctions. Leather is a delicate, living material.
- Always brush your shoes before wearing them. Consider this as indispensable as combing your hair before going out.
- To stop shoes from getting ruined in the rain, protect them with a water-repellent spray: this also works well on suede. Once you get home after a downpour, let your shoes dry out in shoe forms, then give them another spray. These days you can buy excellent, reasonably priced plastic shoe forms, which are more practical than the wooden ones reserved for true shoe lovers. And what about the old trick of stuffing them with newspaper? The shoes dry quickly, but don't reacquire their original shape.
- If a pair of shoes wears out after you've worn them only a few times, don't accept it: take them back to the shop, demanding a repair or substitute. This is your right, especially if you paid a lot for them.
- If a pair of boots you have bought turn out to be unexpectedly too tight on the calves, don't give them away to a skinnier friend. Ask a shoe repair person to stretch the leg.
- As far as sneakers go, there are people who put them in the washing machine, but experts advise washing them with a soft brush and a mixture of water and liquid soap or mild detergent. Marks on the leather trimming can be removed with cotton wool dipped in milk or, in extreme cases, correction fluid.

How a Shoe Is Designed and Produced

There is certainly an artistic element in creating a shoe. Pierre Hardy, a designer for Dior when the *maison* was under Gianfranco Ferré, and since 1990, as a creator for Hermès, actually studied the plastic arts. Famous for his perfectly proportioned heels, he claims they are "able to define the silhouette of a woman, just like the final brushstroke in a painting."

Becoming an accessories designer is not easy. Sara Porro, the thirty-seven-year-old creative force behind Tod's bags and shoes, also has her own line, called *Dove nuotono gli squali,* or Where Sharks Swim. She studied at Milan's Istituto Marangoni and, like everyone else there, thought she would become a clothes designer. By chance, her first job was as assistant to an accessories designer, and thus her career was born. Sara considers herself very lucky; she entered this world at the right time, just when accessories were becoming an important part of fashion. Today those working in her field for the big names are few and highly sought after. But how do you design a shoe?

"Inspiration can come from any source," says Sara. "You have fashion, which means a collection of clothes, that can suggest a trend. Then there is personal research. You study vintage shoes from flea markets, but also apparently completely incongruous objects. In a dog's boutique in New York, I bought some very pretty collars: I just had the feeling they'd stimulate new ideas. A few seasons back, I designed a collection inspired by Lapland; as well as adding a twist to their traditional decorations, I was inspired by the colors and images of the sky there. While this is the cultural aspect of my work, there is also a practical side that consists of field research. I listen very carefully to the women around me, to their enthusiasm for or complaints about any particular model. When I have a picture in my head, when I have chosen the leitmotif of the new collection, then I start designing the 'hero piece' of a series."

Once the design has been approved, it is taken to the company's lastmaker, where a last is created from a piece of wood which will then be covered by leather or preselected materials.

The standard size of the last, equivalent until recently in clothes terms to an Italian 42, or U.S. 10, was a shoe size 36 or a U.S. 6. But as Italian women's height and shoe sizes have grown, this has now become a 37, equivalent to U.S. 6½.

The last is then taken to a heelmaker, where the prototype is made: a minisculpture either in fiberboard or plaster of Paris.

After the last has been approved, work begins on the model. The modelmaker, together with Sara, undertakes necessary modifications. It is at this point that actual "construction" of the shoe begins. The upper, which is the "dress" that covers it, is cut out, and the sole and heel are made; in total, a hundred other single operations are required.

Not bad for an object we walk all over!

International Sizes

Salvatore Ferragamo divided women into three categories according to their foot measurements: Cinderellas, Venuses, and Aristocrats. Cinderellas were those with small feet (continental 37s or U.S. 6 and smaller); Venuses were exact 37s (U.S. 6); while Aristocrats wore 38s, or U.S. 6½ and larger. Venuses, blessed with perfect feet, according to Ferragamo, were the actress Susan Hayworth and the duchess of Windsor, Wallis Simpson. Rita Hayworth was a Venus who wore a wide-fitting 37 (U.S. 6A), while the extremely tall Greta Garbo was an Aristocratic 7AA, and Lauren Bacall, who had very long, somewhat wide feet, was a 9AAA.

When buying shoes abroad, one has to bear in mind certain differences in sizing. Here are some useful examples:

- An Italian or French 37 is the same as an English 4 or an American 6½.

- An Italian or French 38 is the same as an English 5 or an American 7½.
- An Italian or French 39 is the same as an English 6 or an American 8. And so forth.

Health and Shoes:
A Topic That Won't Be
Broached

𝓔ven 𝒩aomi 𝒞ampbell, who has the bearing of a panther, once stumbled and fell on a catwalk because of a pair of shoes that were too high. You need to know how to walk in certain shoes and if you wear these shoes too often, you can risk more than the occasional tumble.

Some experts in podiatry maintain that a "May Damage Your Health" sign, like the warning on cigarette packets, should appear on heels over three and a half inches high.

An exaggeration? Not really. Artificially compressing the extremities causes harm. Chinese women whose feet were bound to stop them from growing suffered severe skeletal problems from osteoporosis to arthritis, as is the case with elderly Western women who spent the 1950s tottering around on the stilettos that were the fashion of the day.

What fate, therefore, lies in store for the bones of this generation who are slaves to even more killer heels? Osteopaths claim it is still too early to tell, but they admit that the construction of today's shoes (softer materials, more care devoted to the anatomical shape of the inner sole) would appear to be less harmful.

In the meantime, however, in order to be able to wear certain kinds of terribly narrow, pointed shoes, many women will do anything, including going under the surgeon's knife.

In New York, in her luxurious Park Avenue clinic, the podiatrist Suzanne Levine operates on six pairs of feet a week at fifty thousand dollars a pop. The most popular operation is the "filing" or, in more severe cases, the elimination, of bunions. Even the Italian TV presenter Paola Barale has admitted to undergoing a similar operation, claiming, "I didn't use to like my toes, but now I can wear any sandals I like."

As for other mini-operations in demand so that one looks better in shoes, these range from ankle and calf liposuction to subcutaneous injections of silicone gel to soften up areas in the foot that rub against shoes that are either too high or too tight. These are the ridiculous excesses of times in which we can't stomach the slightest physical imperfection, or do without the latest fashion. Without being too alarmist, it is still possible to pick up some useful advice from this state of affairs:

Ten Rules for Happy Feet

- Know that as you get older, feet tend to get longer and wider. It's useless trying to squeeze into your usual size 6½; probably, after the age of forty, you'll be a 7½.

- Remember that, whatever your age, Audrey Hepburn advised buying shoes half a size bigger than necessary, as comfort is integral to elegance.

- For the same reason, it is a good idea to buy shoes in the evening, when feet are at their biggest, and never in the morning.

- Whether you're buying heels or flats, never get shoes that aren't instantly comfortable: the "breaking in" myth needs debunking.

- Try not to wear the same pair of shoes for too many days in a row. In fact, ideally you should change them every day so as to avoid the shoes losing their shape, and the feet getting used to a single contour.

- Whenever you get the chance—at home or on the beach—try to walk around barefoot.
- After an evening of walking around on heels, massage the soles of your feet with a tennis ball.
- Look at the feet of your mother and grandmother. Many small deformations are hereditary, and therefore preventable.
- If your feet ache or are often reddened on the sides, find a good podiatrist and visit as often as you would the dentist.
- Whatever kind of shoes you wear and whatever the shape of your feet, accept and love them, pampering them with love and pedicures. Your feet are a pedestal from which arises your beautiful soul.

Epilogue

In the thriller *Blow Fly*, starring the detective Kay Scarpetta (about whom we like everything, beginning with her name) the American writer Patricia Cornwell writes: "For some offenders it's shoes and feet. . . . The shoe itself is sexually arousing to the offender. Frequently he then feels the need to kill the woman wearing the fetish or whose body part is the fetish. Many serial killers got their starts as fetish burglars, going into homes, stealing shoes, underwear, other objects that mean something to them sexually."

It's enough to give you goosebumps. And it might even be true. Come on, girls, let's call a spade a spade here: Would you give up your shoe collection for the abstract fear of a fetishistic killer? No, I thought not.

The biggest nightmare of a shoe-obsessed woman is actually quite different, and is perfectly depicted in a scene of the film *The War of the Roses*. In this scene the husband, played by Michael Douglas, and wife, played by Kathleen Turner, are in the throes of a messy divorce when he picks up one of his wife's shoes and saws off the heels! The exclusively male fear of castration doesn't even come close to this.

Thus, in conclusion, it is fair to assume that if you have either bought or been given this book as a present, and you've read up to this point, you probably own a fair number of shoes. Or would like to. And you often feel guilty because it's never enough. And you often buy shoes that have nothing to do with either your lifestyle or clothes or physical type. Well, cheer up—you're part of a large tribe.

Joan Crawford admitted it: "Shoes are my weakness." She confessed to owning three hundred pairs. Another Hollywood diva, Jayne Mansfield, owned two hundred. Two famous Eves in history were also shoe fanatics: Eva Braun, Adolf Hitler's mistress, and Eva Perón, Argentina's First Lady.

A third, very famous Eve, "Mrs. Adam," is the only woman in history never to have experienced the fantastic thrill of choosing a pair of shoes. We feel for her. We understand why she got chummy with the serpent and how all hell then broke loose. She must have been incandescent with rage upon learning that she was in an earthly paradise without a single shoe shop in the entire neighborhood.

Glossary

BALLERINA FLATS Round-toed shoes with a heel height between 0 and one-half inch, which were inspired by the practice shoes of classical ballerinas and patented in 1957 by Salvatore Ferragamo. They were made famous by legendary actresses such as Audrey Hepburn and Brigitte Bardot.

CAMPARIS Black patent-leather Mary Janes (see below) with a pointed toe and stiletto heel, an important model of the early 1990s by the Spanish designer Manolo Blahnik, revered throughout the world by shoe fanatics.

CAMPERS Round-toed "biscuit shaped" Spanish shoes loved by alternative, antiglobalization youth throughout the world. Some models have a kind of split personality, with different decorations on the left and right foot.

CINDERELLA Protagonist of the fairy tale of the eponymous, much-loved fairy tale. Cinderella has to work as a servant, but in truth she is a girl of noble birth. A prince discovers this is the case thanks to one detail, namely that she is the only girl in the realm who fits into a slipper, which in the Brothers Grimm and Charles Perrault versions is made of glass. In the same Chinese tale it is a golden shoe, while in Giovan Battista Basile's Neapolitan version it is silk. Whatever the case, Cinderella is responsible for associating the shoe with the idea of a magic object, a kind of metaphor for femininity and fragility.

CHANEL SLING-BACK A strappy shoe that leaves the heel exposed, named after its creator, the legendary French designer Coco Chanel.

CROMWELL A high-heeled shoe with a buckle in the front, very fashionable in England toward the end of the nineteenth century. The name derives from a mistaken belief that shoes with large buckles were worn during the times of Oliver Cromwell, a seventeenth-century English politician.

DERBY (OR OXFORD) Lace-up men's shoes (also beloved by many women), often two-toned (known as "spectators"), which were particularly fashionable in the 1920s and 1930s.

ESPADRILLES Canvas summer shoes of Spanish origin with a rope sole. A flat version exists, often worn like a slipper, as well as platforms with laces up to the ankle. Most popular during the 1970s.

KHRUSHCHEV, NIKITA Soviet politician who during a fiery UN session removed one of his shoes and banged it on the table. This story has nothing to do with this book, but I mention it merely to draw attention to the fact that a woman would never have done such a thing.

MARCOS, IMELDA Born in 1929, wife of the ex-dictator of the Philippines, Ferdinand Marcos. She was extremely wealthy and famous for her outrageously lavish lifestyle. She was accused of owning three thousand pairs of shoes, a figure she always denied, claiming it was "only" one thousand and sixty. A woman obsessed with shoes is known as an "Imeldista."

MARY JANES American term for a round-toed shoe with a strap. Its origins lie in the shoes worn by characters in early-twentieth-century comic books, Buster Brown and his little sister, Mary Jane. The rights to the characters were acquired by the Brown Shoe Company, which, under the name Buster Brown, became the most famous American manufacturer of children's shoes.

MORETTI, NANNI Italian film director born in 1953 in Brunico, in the province of Bolzano. Well known for his obsession with shoes, particularly in the film *Bianca* (1984), where there is a famous monologue on the subject: "In the summer of . . . '72, I think it was, some women began to wear Dutch clogs, in white. Had they been to Holland? No idea, but all I know is that a couple of years later, all you could find were imitations: a higher heel, and these hideous metal studs. . . . Though the black ones were nice, very plain looking, a bit scuffed up. They were worn by girls with long blond hair draped over their jumpers, dressed in blue drainpipes and red knee-high socks."

OXFORDS (SEE DERBYS)

PENNY LOAFERS "Loafers" or "college shoes" are an urban version of the loafer. The name penny loafer derives from the habit, fashionable among American students in the 1950s, of slipping a decorative penny into the front "keeper" strap.

SABOT Generic French term for clog. In Italian it also refers to all slip-on shoes, be they high or low, which in English are called mules.

SABRINA HEEL A kind of low, slightly curved, very feminine heel, inspired by Audrey Hepburn in Billy Wilder's 1954 film *Sabrina*.

Sneakers All sports shoes, be they of the fashionable or technical variety.

Sperry Top-Siders The first yachting shoe as we know it today. This invention got its name from the American Paul Sperry (1895–1982). Born in Connecticut, he was a keen sailor who created an antislip rubber sole with zigzag grooves inspired by the paws of Prince, his cocker spaniel.

Wedges Platform shoes that were very fashionable during World War II, reappearing in different forms throughout successive decades.

Bibliography

Bowd, Emma. *Mad About Shoes.* Ryland Peters & Small, 2006.

Brubach, Holly. *A Dedicated Follower of Fashion.* Phaidon, 1999.

Clarke Keogh, Pamela. *Audrey Style.* HarperCollins, 1999.

Cornwell, Patricia. *Blow Fly.* Putnam, 2003.

Fox, Patty. *Star Style: Hollywood Legends as Fashion Icons.* Angel City Press, 1995.

Garcia, Bobbito. *Where'd You Get Those? New York City's Sneaker Culture 1960–1987.* Testify Books, 2005.

Klein, Naomi. *No Logo: No Space, No Choice, No Jobs.* Picador, 2002.

Morris, Desmond. *The Naked Woman: A Study of the Female Body.* Thomas Dunne, 2005.

O'Keeffe, Linda. *Shoes: A Celebration of Pumps, Sandals, Slippers, and More.* Workman, 1996.

Pratt, Lucy, and Linda Wolley. *Shoes.* Victoria & Albert Museum, 1999.

Quart, Alissa. *Branded: The Buying and Selling of Teenagers.* Basic Books, 2004.

Reilly, Maureen, and John Klycinski. *Hot Shoes: One Hundred Years.* Schiffer, 1998.

Steele, Valerie. *Shoes: A Lexicon of Style.* Scriptum, 2006.

Tobias, Tobi. *Obsessed by Dress.* Beacon, 2000.

Worsley, Harriet. *Decades of Fashion.* Konemann, 2000.

Acknowledgments

My thanks to the people who have helped me in the writing of this book, in particular Sara Porro, Fulvio Zendrini, Stefania Ricci, and Mrs. Wanda Ferragamo.

Thanks to Nicola Salerno for *Elio's Song*.

Thanks to *Vanity Fair*'s editor in chief, Carlo Verdelli, and associate editor, Christina Lucchini; but also to Enrica, Bombs, Tissy, Barbarina, and in general to all the editorial team at *Vanity Fair*, who have had to put up with me droning on about shoes for all these months.

Thanks to Maria Laura Giovagnini for daily moral support, as well as to my editor, Marcella Meciani, who, as they always say in these cases (though it's really true!), never stopped believing in me.

Thanks to my mother and all my girlfriends with whom I have shared many truly epic shoe moments over the last twenty years. From 1980s cone heels to the bamboo clogs of 2002, from French pedicures to buying shoes on the Internet, it has to be said that we never wanted for anything, at least as far as our feet were concerned.

Special thanks to Gianmaria, for the expression (irresistible and comical) that he assumes each time I buy a new pair of shoes.

Last but not least, to Giulia Cogoli, who, apart from having many merits as a friend, introduced me to Marcella, Sara, and Gianmaria.

About the Author
and the Illustrator

PAOLA JACOBBI is a journalist and special correspondent for Italian *Vanity Fair*. She lives in Milan.

SUJEAN RIM is an illustrator whose work is often seen on the website DailyCandy. She lives in New York City.